TUNDRA TAILS

A RIVETING STORY ABOUT A WOMAN WITH COURAGE AND A SPIRIT OF ADVENTURE LIVING IN ALASKA

PENNY NICKLE

Wasteland Press

www.wastelandpress.net
Shelbyville, KY USA

Tundra Tails:
A Riveting Story About A Woman with Courage
And A Spirit of Adventure Living in Alaska
by Penny Nickle

First Printing – November 2012
ISBN: 978-1-60047-777-5

Printed in the U.S.A.

0   1   2   3   4   5   6   7

SPECIAL THANKS
to

Don Johnson	Warren Johnson
Allen Nelson	Laurie Johnson
Arlene Nelson	Theo Chesley
John Guidos	Trina Doyle
Little Allen	Leona Nelson
Maxi Johnson	Dailey & Paul

And all of the other wonderful people that I have grown to know and love. Without them this adventure would not have been possible or as enjoyable.

I would like to dedicate this book to a very loyal and
loving little buddy,

Cowboy

Rest in peace my faithful friend.
We will meet again.

Cowboy 1991-1998

FOREWORD

My son and my daughter were grown and had moved out of the home. They stay busy with their lives so when I was offered a job working on the highways of Oregon, flagging traffic, I accepted it.

That is where I met Rick. He was a surveyor for the State of Oregon, Highway division.

From the beginning, the conversations always drifted in the direction of Alaska, as he was seriously planning to move there.

From the beginning, I considered the thought and one year later, I was on my way.

We sold or gave away all of our belongings except for survival gear; tools and camping equipment and left Portland Oregon heading north in May of 1994. We camped throughout Canada and Alaska until we reached the end of the Sterling Highway in Homer Alaska.

The summer and fall were spent camping mostly on the Kasilof River and at various other locations around the Kenai Peninsula from May until October when we went to Bear Lake Lodge. That was the icing on a cake that I will hunger for and treasure, as long as I live.

TABLE OF CONTENTS

1

The Adventure Begins

September 17, 1994

I awoke today to heavy winds and rain but prepared for the journey as was scheduled. The summer camp, on the Kasilof River was where I have called home for the last six months while camping in a 1960's pop up tent trailer.

Spending the summer on the banks of the Kasilof River has been wonderful. The peace, sound, and sights are amazing. Various birds are thick in the sky and on the river banks. They include a pair of Bald Eagles along with their nest. Watching the pair of eagles fish and protect the nest has been captivating. Thousands of Arctic Terns hovered above the water fishing for the newly hatched fish. Constant beautiful screeches and songs from the different species of birds enthrall me.

Several moose young and old have wandered nearby and several times crossed the river here at camp. Most often just stomping and crashing through the heavy foliage can be heard as the moose pass.

The Kasilof River supports unbelievable salmon fishing which all made for a dream summer. But with fall upon us, and the temperature dropping, we needed to make plans to go indoors.

The Kenai Peninsula is very seasonal and the season had just ended. Many businesses have closed and tourists have left the state.

We began searching for a place to care take for the winter answering ads in the Anchorage Newspaper. After several meetings with two Kenai residents, Don and Warren Johnson, the owners of a lodge located on the Alaskan Peninsula, a winter position was secured. We were headed to the Aleutian Mountain Range on the Bearing Sea side, to spend eight months in solitude at a place named "Bear Lake Lodge."

I tried to think of everything that we might need or want while living in remote Alaskan Bush, and shipped what we could, to the lodge ahead of time. Craft materials, books, puzzles, writing paper, and lots of postage stamps, were purchased. As the time approached for our scheduled departure our camp was secured and we spent the last days in a neighbor's camp trailer on the Kasilof River. We took a final drive into the town of Soldotna for an indoor shower and also to drive to the Soldotna City Airport for a conformation with Clearwater Air, the air charter service that would be flying us to the lodge tomorrow.

While we were talking with our pilot, the phone rang and it was a lady named, Kat, calling from Nelson Lagoon, a small village along the Bearing Sea, about 40 fly miles from Bear Lake Lodge. She was relaying a message to us from Warren who was at the lodge; the call was put on speakerphone so we could all hear the conversation, it was our first taste of life in the bush.

While we were talking a static, crackling, sound came from the background as we heard Warren's voice calling Kat over the marine radio. We listened as Warren told Kat that it was too windy to consider flying us in right now and the forecast for the next day was the same. We were instructed to put off our departure for a few days to allow the weather to calm. The plans changed in an instant. No one got excited, the weather dictates the activity. We gave the pilot a message phone number for us, bought a few groceries, and headed back to the Kasilof River to wait.

The orange and yellow fall colors of the leaves still dancing on the trees showed off brilliant against the clear bright blue sky. It was peaceful, yet the gentle breeze seemed to hold a warning message with it. Frosts were covering everything nightly now and it felt like snow could be falling soon.

Settled back into the camp trailer, I bundled up, made a cup of tea and returned to the map to study the route that we would be flying. Only a few hours passed when we heard a vehicle approaching; our message person drove over giving us the message that the weather had changed and our departure was on again, for tomorrow.

2

Bear Lake Lodge

9/18/94

Finally the big day arrived. With great excitement and anticipation I awoke often through the night getting out of bed at 5:30 am. The night had remained calm and clear. I wondered if the weather had also stayed calm at the lodge. I savored the moments knowing they will be my last at this wonderful campsite on the Kasilof River. As I sat outside, drinking coffee, waiting for the sun to rise above the horizon, steam rolled softly off of the river while frost glittered in the light of the full moon. The scenery was dramatic and exhilarating. The sound of the water flowing over the rocks and splashing against the river banks was calming and brought peace of mind for me, yet even with all this around me my mind was raging with wild excitement as I carefully considered that this is my last chance to change my mind and stay in the safety of civilization. As the sun came up, all of my fears and concerns were washed away with the wonders of the adventure that lay ahead.

We drove into Soldotna, stopped for a local newspaper, one last fast food fix, and headed down the long, winding road that follows the Kenai River to the Soldotna Airport. We pulled up to the Clearwater Hanger and I was delighted to see that Don Johnson, the man with the dream and builder of the lodge, is present to see us off.

We had gone to Don's home several times to talk with him about the history of the lodge and what to expect. Each word he spoke infiltrated as I wanted to learn everything possible from the man with the highest level of experience and wisdom about "Bear Lake Lodge." Don's health was failing and he was now confined to a wheelchair. I could see the longing and the sparkle in his eyes when he spoke about Bear Lake. Two of his three children, Warren and

Laurie, had taken over the responsibilities of the lodge a few years ago. Don's voice cracked as he spoke with passion. He watched every move while the Cessna 207 was being loaded while he spoke. Don had flown countless trips across Cook Inlet and through the Aleutian Mountains and knew what lied ahead for us, we did not. He could also see the anticipation in my eyes, and said, "Don't you worry now sweetie. He's a good pilot he hasn't crashed yet!" We laughed and he continued to tease me with warnings while we watched as fresh fruit, milk, vegetables, a live jalapeno pepper plant, along with our belongings, were thoughtfully placed in the plane.

Finally, it was time for us to board, so I buckled up behind the pilot with my faithful dog and companion, Cowboy, at my side.

We taxied to the runway after clearing "take off" with the tower, and climbed up and over the land that I had become familiar with on the ground. I followed our route with a map as we flew over the gray waters of the Cook Inlet and entered into the world of Lake Clark Pass. The passage is carved through the rugged Aleutian Mountain Range.

Aleutian Mountain Range

As we flew into the gap of the mountains I was in complete awe by the beauty of the blue glaciers, jagged rock formations, and the silent valleys down below.

Lake Clark Pass

All of the dazzling colors of fall were showing as the red and green tundra lined the shores of Lake Clark. The glacier water in the lake was a beautiful deep shade of turquoise.

I continued studying the map as we flew over "no mans" land and made our way through the pass. We left the tree line behind as we flew over the Village of King Salmon, continuing past Mount Iliamna, where the famous Katmai National Park could be seen in the distance.

After we left the mountains behind, we flew along the west side of the Alaska Peninsula following the shores of the Bearing Sea.

The sea is gray and rough with black volcanic sand shorelines. We spotted several herds of caribou upon vast miles of tundra while flock after flock of birds, could be seen as they dealt with their own migrations. We flew over Cape Seniavin and I was delighted at the sight of a large walrus herd wallowing on the sand and swimming in the sea! It was an amazing sight!

Walrus

We followed the coastline, flying low, and scanning the beaches for treasures. Dead walrus are very desirable for valuable ivory tusks and they do not lie on the beaches very long as people constantly search for them. I was relieved to see only live ones, as for me, that was the treasure.

About twenty miles out from the lodge, the rain and wind started. The pilot continued to follow the shoreline of the Bearing Sea until we reached the mouth of Bear River, then turned the plane following Bear River to the lodge. My stomach began to jump with eagerness the closer we became. All I had been thinking about is this day not knowing what I am really getting myself into and now it is all happening fast. As the lodge came in to sight in the distance, tears welled up in my eyes. I viewed pictures and read all of the information I could find about the area and history, but nothing prepared me for the beauty of paradise, in experiencing the lodge with my own eyes.

Bear Lake Lodge

The lodge is located at the mouth of Bear Lake, where the waters form Bear River, which flows to the Bearing Sea. Bear Lake is large; seven miles long and three miles wide. Bear Lake is also very deep and cold. Mountains and hillsides provide incredible 360 degree views. There are mountains to the south, east, and west but to the north, the terrain flattens out into miles of swampy tundra. We circled the 1200-foot gravel airstrip before making the final approach to land. Upon landing, Warren was the first to greet the plane and welcome us in. A fabulous hot meal was waiting and after eating, our things were unloaded and the process of unpacking began.

The lodge is just wonderful. I feel very comfortable and the cooking facilities are fabulous. Several pantries and freezers are stocked with more food than I can imagine and eating will not be the challenge this winter. There is a daylight basement and directly above it hosts a lounge. The lounge overlooks Bear Lake, the mouth of Bear River, and a view downstream for as far as I can see. The sights are hypnotizing and very peaceful yet powerful. I never want to leave.

The lounge is filled with artifacts and fascinating treasures that keep the past alive. There are many varieties of mounted animals and approximately thirty sets of walrus skulls and tusks. There are also many sets of brown bear skulls that catch my attention every time I enter the room. I am amazed with the discovery that each bear skull is extremely different. The jaw line and teeth structures are individual clearly revealing that every animal has their own look.

Bear skulls on rafter

I love the peaceful feeling in the lounge. I stood and looked out of the picture windows watching as Silver Salmon rolled in the river tempting me to grab a fishing pole and try my luck. Instead my eyes continued to wander while absorbing the surroundings, which have me completely intrigued. The amount of work, patience, and dedication it would have taken to build such a palace, here in the middle of nowhere is unbelievable. All materials had to be flown in. The small airstrip limits the size of planes that can land which also means that countless trips were flown.

Four seasonal cannery workers from Port Moller were flown in for the day to enjoy some good "Bear Lake hospitality." They fished most of the day then told stories in the lounge this evening about their adventure of working the long hard salmon season they had endured. The men are flying out tomorrow, returning to their homes in various locations throughout the United States. Their adventure was ending, creating a beginning to ours.

The bush planes of Bear Lake buzzed in and out of the lodge all day taking people out and bringing supplies in. A full course turkey dinner was prepared with peach pie for desert. The evening was spent in the lounge entertaining us with tales of the past and warnings for the future. It was fascinating and I will never forget the impact of that night. Around midnight I decided to spend some time in my room getting settled so I excused myself and said my good nights to everyone. As I did, I was offered a chaperone to walk me to the guest quarters but I declined trying to be brave while understanding I am in danger of bears. No one insisted, however, I was reminded about going past or around blind corners in between the lodge and bunkhouse because of the bears. I listened while thinking I should have chosen the chaperone. Heading out the door of the main lodge I stomped my feet as I walked and talked to Cowboy as we followed the path, past one building, out in to the open and over to the bunkhouse. I was so relieved to be inside I felt weak, but at least safe, I hoped. I was the only one in the building and it felt quite eerie. I looked around at all of the treasures again before heading up stairs to my room.

The building consists of guestrooms and bathroom facilities on the main floor, including a recreation room with a pool table, dartboard, TV, and VCR. There are also laundry facilities. Upstairs is a second recreation room filled with shelves of books and jig saw puzzles. The large picture windows on the upper floor provide outstanding views. Continuing down the hall is the staff quarters and Warren's private room.

I arraigned a few things then snuggled into the comfort of my bed, while my mind raced with all that was happening or about to happen to me. As I lay there I heard bears outside in the distance. The young cubs were baying to their mother. It was spine-chilling yet so wonderful and thrilling. One of the many moments I will never forget.

9/19

I awoke today and the weather was nice. The winds have calmed and I slept very sound. Breakfast was served and we all enjoy the social time that accompanies the meals in the dining room. After breakfast the planes were up and flying as the last of the guests were flown out. With the final load of clients boarded in the plane the remaining staff sighed with relief.

I went for a walk up the rocky beach of the lakeshore but only as far as the first curve. I was too nervous to go beyond the point of losing sight of the lodge. There are a lot of feathers from various birds and I am excited to start collecting them. After my walk, most of the day was spent relaxing and getting familiar with the surroundings.

The sight of the fish rolling was more than I could stand so I got my pole and headed out. The rain and wind kicked up and after losing two salmon I called it a good day of fishing and went inside to dry out and warm up.

The lodge has a satellite dish, which means there is a link to the outside world. The channels come from Denver. Having TV will be a huge help for the long winter ahead, however, it is powered by a generator, which cannot be running all the time, so watching TV will be limited.

Football is a favorite pass time here at the lodge and since today is Monday night everyone gathered around the TV and joined in on the weekly betting pool. We put in twenty dollars along with the others and drew number seven which turned out to be a good draw, winning three of the four quarters, turning the twenty dollar investment into one hundred and seventy five. It was a good time; even with the harassing we took.

The wind is blowing hard and bringing in rain. I spent my second night drifting to sleep while the rain beat and the wind howled against the windows.

9/20

It stormed heavy all night bringing wind gusts up to sixty miles an hour. I was wakeful most of the night but did not mind as I am fascinated by the severity of the storms. There is a digital wind and temperature meter located in the dining room. I find it intriguing to follow, which will assist in keeping track of the conditions outside. I spent much of the day in the lounge with my eyes glued to the spotting scope searching for wildlife while engrossed in the picturesque surroundings. The scope is like huge binoculars, proving a close up view with both eyes. I spend countless time looking through them. I was beside myself with excitement when I finally spotted my first bear. The sow had twins and it was beyond thrilling to watch them play as mama bear led the way along the shores of the lake. I watched the three bears until they vanished out of sight. Even though they were quite a distance away, I was ecstatic.

Later this afternoon a disturbing radio call came in that a pilot with passengers on board from Clearwater Air had failed to return to Soldotna, after being in this area yesterday. The atmosphere changed immediately from light hearted and laughing to somber and concerned. No distress signal had been sent out but the news had everyone feeling uneasy. I listened in silence as the two remaining pilots at the lodge, Warren and John, discussed the situation and painstaking concluded that wind conditions were too severe to fly a search, which made the situation even more difficult for us all to endure while the time passed and the radio remained silent. Everyone went to bed tonight without the usual social time in the lounge.

9/21

As I lay in bed, waking this morning, I realized that it was calm. The storm had passed and the wind had stopped. I jumped out of bed and headed for the dining room. Warren was already up and watching for the weather report. He finished his coffee and began his preparations to fly. Before leaving he instructed John to continue flying in firewood and diesel fuel from Port Moller. The firewood that was being flown in is from repairs done on the docks at Port Moller. The docks were originally built during WWII. There is a wood stove in the lounge for heat and a diesel burning heating stove in the dining room. The cook stoves, hot water heater, and clothes dryers, operate by propane. The electricity is provided by generators, which also run on diesel. When we are here alone, we will move a bed into the dining area and only heat that space. We can burn a fire in the woodstove to enjoy the lounge occasionally but there is not enough wood to keep it going very much of the time. All the other buildings will be shut down and winterized so pipes will not freeze.

The boxes that we shipped arrived today so we spent most of the time unpacking and organizing. The atmosphere was solemn as everyone tried to keep busy while time slowly passed as we anxiously awaited a radio call from Warren or someone.

The radio remained quiet until a call came in from Allen and Arlene Nelson, from Nelson Lagoon. The Aleut Native Village is 40 fly miles away. They are to flying over today, spend the night so we can get acquainted and discuss the winter plans. They will be our outside connection, bringing in supplies, mail, and back up support for any problems that might occur. Within a few hours Allen and Arlene arrived. It was pleasurable and comforting to meet them. I am captivated with them both and I feel we will become good friends.

I could not sit still or stand the sight of the fish rolling any longer so I went outside to give the fish another chance to live. This time I landed four nice silver salmon, saying to myself, "Now this is fishing!"

Finally a radio call came in from Warren; he had found the grounded plane. Everyone on board was fine and we all cheered! The spirit of the lodge came back to life once again. The pilot landed on the shoreline of the Bearing Sea damaging the prop as he touched down. Six people were on board and had just spent the night in a very dangerous and uncomfortable situation. They were equally excited to have Warren show up and he was able to make arraignments for a new prop to be flown in for them that same day. They were cold and concerned and still had to wait longer. What a story they would have to tell when they arrived home. The danger for them was that the waves could come in far enough to reach the plane and they are sitting in Brown Bear country with nowhere to hide. After Warren accomplished what he could for them, he flew, while they waited. The pilot is a man who only has one leg so hopefully the tide and the bears will cooperate, until the new prop arrives.

Two guides and the housekeeper are still at the lodge and decided to take the skiff down the river for one last look at the abandoned Aleut village on the mouth of Bear River, where it flows into the Bearing Sea. When they did not arrive back to the lodge for dinner, Warren asked John, to take the super cub and fly the river looking for them. I had already expressed my desires about flying so John asked me if I would like to tag along. Needless to say, I was ready and standing at the plane before he could change his mind. A super cub is made by Piper and is a two-passenger plane that seats the passenger behind the pilot. The cabin is small and narrow allowing the controls to be operated by either the front or back seat pilot. The plane is very light with a covering of cloth. My description of a super cub is a flying dress. They are amazing planes capable of taking off and landing in limited areas because they are able to fly at a very slow speed.

We secured ourselves and up into the air we went. About seven miles downriver a spike camp is placed for hunters and or survival, which was where we spotted the skiff beached on the shore. We circled low and slow and I was surprised when John landed on such a short stretch of beach. The boat had motor trouble caused by water in the fuel. Gas was drained from the plane and put into fuel cans for the boat. (super cubs fly on gas not airplane fuel) The two guides were working on the motor when we landed but the housekeeper was inside the cabin warming up. John asked me to go to the cabin to see if she wanted to fly back with us or finish the trip in the boat. In order to get to the cabin I had to work my way through a willow and alder thicket, which had me feeling uneasy. I was surprised at how tall and dense the thickets are, there are bear tracks everywhere and it was beginning to get dark. I was relieved to get inside the cabin and I took a good look at supplies. There is a Coleman stove and lantern, two bunks with dry sleeping bags, canned foods, and kitchen utensils.

The three explorers were wet and cold. Again the situation reminded me about how different life will be for us once the planes leave. There will be no one to come looking in the case we do not return to the lodge. At that moment, I fully understood that every move we make will have to be with careful planning and caution. It could mean life or death.

With the boat engine running again, Becky chose to fly back to the lodge and loaded into the baggage compartment behind the second seat in the cub. We lifted off of the gravel beach rising back up into the air in the land of never ending wonderment. We wing waved at the two guys who were back in the river and on their way upstream to the lodge. From the air I could see for miles and the country is very barren. It looks impossible to walk very far due to the amount of backwaters and tundra swamp land. Without flying, there was no way in or out which is a peculiar feeling.

9/22

The next couple of days were spent preparing for the groups departure and our stay. Freezers were condensed and it was comforting to see exactly what was available to us. Moose burger is made here and it is very good. There are steaks, king crab, shrimp, halibut, salmon, and even lobster all vacuumed sealed.

Bread and pastries are made from scratch and there are plenty of supplies for that. Several pantries are stocked with canned and dried foods, so in that respect I liked the kind of roughing it we were going to be doing.

The biggest treat of the day was watching the bears. Several bears were spotted throughout the day as they walked the shoreline of the lake occasionally stopping to catch and eat salmon. Around 8:30 pm three bears were spotted coming towards the lodge so everyone scrambled to gather up any outside garbage, close all doors, and buckle down in preparation of the arrival of the great bruins. Even though the bears turned and did not come to the lodge it was exciting! Given the amount of bear tracks I have been seeing it is apparent that I can expect plenty of visitors.

3

Left Alone

9/23/94

The morning came that we were to be left alone. Last minute instructions were given, final questions and concerns were discussed as the planes were loaded, then they taxied up the gravel runway and lifted up into the air. We stood at the edge of the airstrip watching, waving, and listening, until the last plane could no longer be seen or heard. We turned to each other but no words were spoken. We both understood the realization that we had just been left out here alone, in the middle of nowhere, and for the most part, on our own for eight months. From here out our lives will depend on wise decisions and each other. I have never experienced responsibility or emotion so powerful and it is a mixture of excitement and fright.

9/24

The last few days have been spent settling in and getting familiar with the day-to-day life and duties of survival. I have been walking daily but cannot get very far because of the waters and swamp that surround us. There is red mud that makes a huge mess if you step in it over the top of your boots. One of many lessons I have learned.

My latest bit of education was learning how to operate the 5000-watt generator. It is turned on for a few hours during the day then shut off in the late afternoon to conserve the precious diesel fuel. When we shut the large generator off, we start a 650-watt portable generator that runs on gas and sits outside on the porch. It is noisy but powers the TV and one lamp. I find it exciting yet frightening to go out on the porch and shut the generator off. I can feel eyes watching me.

9/25

I am spotting bears daily now as they roam about preparing for their long winter that lay ahead for them. Feeding is their main concern and objection and I am very impressed with their ability to move so swiftly, yet gracefully, while they catch fish. The difference between a Grizzly Bear and a Brown Bear is that the Brown Bear live by the sea and eat fish while, Grizzly Bears live inland and forage more on rodents, berries and roots. The bears use their front paws like hands and once they have a grip on something it does not get away. I have made a note of that.

9/27

It was an exciting night as I bolted awake at the sound of Parti-girl's (the resident, Cocker Spaniel) barking and constant boofing. She refused to stop and as we lay there trying to sleep I grew annoyed until I heard it too. A loud thump outside the kitchen window! I jumped up, grabbed a flashlight, and headed for the window. If the window would have been opened I could have reached out and touched a mighty Alaskan Brown Bear! I watched the bears mingle around, searching for something to eat until they wandered away baying and snorting to each other. One cub chewed on the wooden fence then both cubs walked out onto the dock while mama bear patiently waited on the beach as the cubs explored. The moon was bright and I could see clearly while they worked themselves downstream and out of sight.

The fishing remains good during the day and the yard seems to come alive at night with curious and passing visitors.

9/28

The bears are coming nightly now and sleep goes by the way side. I spotted three caribou across the river feeding in the tundra while working their way north. In the distance a large bull was leading another small herd and I watched them make their way towards the first three cows. The herds will probably join up with the bull.

9/30

I am getting more comfortable with the bears and have started a game with them and the flashlight. The cubs do not like it and run when I shine it at them but always come back. I am finding that quite frequently I have strange dreams after the bears have been here.

10/1

Our first day of mail delivery was exciting. Allen flew in with his daughter, Leona, and little Allen his nephew. He radioed first to see what the conditions are at the lodge so with the forewarning that people were coming I baked a pie and had plenty of fresh coffee, in hopes of persuading them to stay awhile. We had been alone for almost two weeks.

While they were here we had the first snowfall of the season. We watched the large snowflakes rejoicing in the beauty upon us. It was great fun sharing stories and the laughter. They brought life to the lodge. The coffee and pie were enjoyed but when the clouds cleared, it was time for our guests to leave. Again, I stood alongside the airstrip as the plane lifted up and flew away until I could no longer see or hear the buzz of the plane. I spent most of the evening with the magazines and catalogs that had been delivered. We also have some fresh produce, which is a real treat and rare commodity.

4

Bears

10/2/94

I have been getting out and walking everyday and seeing a lot of bears. They mosey along feeding, while working their way south to the head of the lake. That is where they will climb the mountains to sleep for the coldest part of the winter. I spotted the largest bear that I have seen yet. He is massive and supported a large hump on his shoulders. I glued my eyes to the spotting scope while I watched him work his way down the shoreline as the younger bears scattered to get out of his way. At one point, it appeared that there was going to be a confrontation but at the last minute the younger bear had the respect for the big guy and veered away. The huge bruin clearly showed his alpha position and domain. It was very exciting to see such an impressive animal and now I know the difference between a big bear and a really big bear! Eagles congregate here for winter-feeding and more birds are spotted each day. As I walked today there were eagles perched in every direction that I looked.

Birds of prey are a huge interest to us as Rick is an experienced falconer which has interested and educated me.

10/3

Last night after it became dark the bears were so heavy around the lodge that they surrounded us. No matter which window I looked out I would see bears. I will definitely be staying in tonight!

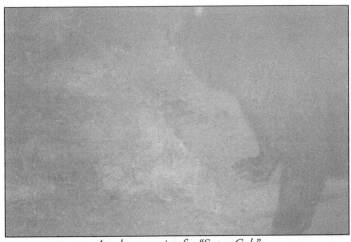

Another meaning for "Super Cub"

10/4

I hardly see Rick anymore. He is irritated at the bears for disturbing his sleep instead of enjoying them and goes up into the lounge to sleep. I have asked him to stay with me, stating that it gets intimidating being alone and on the same level as the bears, but his reply was for me to sleep with the rifle. Our winter space had the only heat so I wanted to stay on the ground level which also allowed me to experience the adventure.

Tonight I was afraid to go out on the porch and turn the generator off so I decided to allow it run out of gas. At 3 am it was still running and I was tired of waiting for it to stop so I worked up the nerve to step outside and turned it off. I ran back in laughing and jumped onto the bed looking at the rifle for comfort as I flew by. It was only minutes later that I heard the bears outside. They were there while I was there and the thought made my hair stand up on my neck. Time passed while I laid there a bit shaky listening to the bears mingle outside the windows. Eventually I calmed enough to get up and look out the windows hoping to locate who is here and where they are. The same sow with the two cubs that are becoming regulars were right outside the kitchen window. The drain from the kitchen empties the gray water into a 55-gallon drum that is buried in the ground and from there the wastewater leaches out under- ground. No matter what precautions are taken the bears find a way to get into the wastewater drum and love to drink the gray liquid. I opened the window quietly without any of the bears noticing. The two cubs were drinking from the barrel and mama bear was rolling on the ground scratching her back. All of a sudden I yelled,"GET OUT OF HERE!" One cub squealed and took off running while the other cub fell into the barrel splashing the stinky gray water all over him and the side of the house. The sow jumped up and took two swift strides away from the lodge then stood up on her hind legs and looked right into my eyes. She was only a few feet from me and the moment was intense. She finally went back down on all fours and ran to catch up with her fleeing babies. Until then I was thinking perhaps I had made a huge mistake with my actions, especially staring back at her, but my fear turned to relief after they were gone. Again, I was safe and back in bed. Re-runs of the experience kept racing through my mind and eventually I got a laugh out of the fact that I had the rare experience of scaring a bear. Needless to say, I did not sleep much after that.

10/5

The days are spent eating, watching for animals, and learning the bear habits. They are constantly on the move and feeding. Each set of bears have their own routine. I recognize the difference in them assisting me in what to expect them to do. I do not take them for granted. They are a mighty hunter and I never forget that. After the bears hibernate I will find something else to write about but for now that is the main topic in my life. I am still seeing a lot of bears everyday but the big excitement came when a sow and four cubs showed up!

Sow and four cubs

I know four cubs are rare and it is a special treat to get the opportunity to watch them attempt to imitate their mother as she works her way along the shores of the river. She fishes and shares her catch with the cubs, studying them fascinates me. The cubs are big and must have been born last year. This will be the last winter their mother will keep them so they have a lot to learn. Most of what the cubs seem to be interested in is playing. They have their own version of tag and they wrestle and snort. They like to take off running then stop on a dime, turn, and go the other way. It makes me want to go out and play with them. They must be getting plenty to eat, as they are not too interested in what mom provides for them. They would rather play. Nothing goes to waste though, as the eagles, ravens, and magpies follow the bears cleaning up every scrap left behind. I watched them until they were out of sight then I went outside to shut off the main generator, which is a distance from the lodge. Upon exiting the shed I realized that the sow and four cubs had circled back around and stood between the lodge and me. I did not take a rifle out with me, as I had been instructed to do, and I now regretted that fact. I watched the sow dig roots and eat them. The cubs still only seemed interested in playing and after about a half an hour of being pinned in the shed the bears moved on and I hurried back into the safety of the lodge.

10/6

Today we decided to do some target practice to see how the rifles fire, which ones we are comfortable with and if we could hit what we are aiming at. While we practiced at the targets I hoped that we would never have to shoot anything. I have decided however, to carry a rifle with me when I am outside. I guess it brings some comfort, along with the sore shoulder. I have been walking up the beach of the lake going farther each time I go out. Today I climbed the hillside that separates the lake from the valley and sat on the top of the ridge for a long time enjoying the view and the tranquility. The dogs stay busy with their noses to the ground. The mountain formations are very rugged yet the calming effect of the snow and the beautiful shade of glacier ice tug at me. I was surprised at the way I had to fight the urge to go closer.

While gazing around I spotted the caribou, after counting them concluded that the three cows had joined up with the bull and his harem. They continue to stay busy feeding on lichen grown on the tundra. While the caribou grazed they stayed alert and constantly on the move. The snow level is dropping on the mountains and hillsides, and the animals know what all of this means. Their energy and concentration strictly goes into preparation for the long hard winter that Alaska supports.

10/7

The sow and four cubs are hanging in the area and I am spotting them daily. I watched as the cubs followed mom along the airstrip and over to the river. They crossed the shallows of the river and after it felt safe I set out to follow their tracks. In doing so, I soon realized that I had made a big mistake. I did not count the bears as they crossed the river and one of the cubs had stayed on this side. In fact, as I came over a small knob on the riverbank I realized that a cub was right below me. I crouched down and stayed motionless. The sow had spotted me and was now pacing back and forth on the other side of the river clearly nervous while she talked with her cub. The cub finally ran down stream in a panic, located the exact spot that the others had crossed, and plunged into the water swimming to the safety of his mom. At that point my fear turned to fun, even though my heart was still pounding while I waited until they all ran away before I made my move for the lodge.

Cub swimming across Bear River

10/8-9

This morning, we awoke to snow at ground level. I am usually the one to go outside and turn the generator on in the morning and off in the evening. Several times I have found myself not only with bears in the distance, but on all sides of me. The bears are focused while they fish and walk the land. So far, the bears seem to be unimpressed with my presence. We all just go about our business. I do of course give them all right of ways if I am outside that is.

The mornings are welcomed and as the sun came up around 9 am. A fresh blanket of snow glittered in the daylight. What a lovely contrast against the bright blue color of the sky. After each new snowfall I bundle up and head out looking for tracks to see who has been around. I am fascinated in finding and following all tracks but I am mostly interested in bear tracks. I follow them trying to learn about habits and behavior. I spotted the sow and two cubs down river at the Fish and Game cabin and I laughed as she stood up on her hind legs and scratched her back on the corner of the cabin. Pieces of wood began to brake off as she rubbed. Occasionally she would turn around and bite at the wood. The fun stopped when the bear began tearing the cabin apart. The bears can be so destructive. She did a large amount of damage just scratching her back.

The bears are very easy to spot now as their brown color contrasts against the snow. If Parti-girl notices a bear, she runs with all her might, which is still very slow, and chases them barking wildly as she runs right at them! The first few times I saw her do this I was terrified that a bear was going to take a swat at her, but to my amazement, the bears run. I suspect they do not understand size.

Our second mail delivery came in along with a letter from my daughter, Cherry. It was nice to have a link with the family and the outside world. Life is taking a whole new meaning here at the lodge. Some things I once took for granted are now extremely important to me, while other things I thought important, now are not.

10/10

I have been having good luck fishing. Along with the salmon I am catching, I am landing some large Dolly Varden. We have enough fish smoked and canned to last the winter so I release all fish that are caught. I never thought I would see that day.

Between the bears appearing at night and the dogs barking at the bears it is impossible to get a goodnight sleep. I am used to Rick sleeping upstairs, and except for the company of the animals, I am feeling alone.

Rick decided to try his luck at trapping and within 10 minutes of setting the traps, he was successful. He caught Cowboy. Fortunately the traps are small and do not have teeth, so as Cowboy screamed and jumped about like a scalded cat, he freed himself before I could get my boots on and get outside to help him.

10/11

I am getting tired from lack of sleep so I decided to sleep upstairs myself to see if the dogs would remain quiet only to be awakened around midnight with Rick out on the deck shooting off fireworks. I could not believe it as I was finally sleeping so sound. Highly irritated, I laid there considering hibernation with the bears.

The bears bayed most of the night after the firework display was over so after giving up the idea of sleeping I arose, built a fire, watched and waited for daylight to come.

As the sun came up on the hillside I have a clear vision of the world that is alive and busy all around me. Bears are everywhere I look. I spotted a bird flying in the direction of the lodge. With pure excitement the large bird flew close enough for me to see that it was a falcon! It was thrilling as I watched him hover high above the ground then with swift speed, dive straight down like a bolt of lightning when he spotted a target. It was an awesome sight as the falcon hunted the tundra across the river. I remained fixed on him until he flew back up lake in the same direction he had come from. I will never forget the feeling I had this morning as I watched the world around me. All I kept thinking was how much I love this place.

10/12

Last night something much larger than Cowboy was caught in Rick's trap. It was a bear cub. Curiosity got the best of the cub and as the trap snapped shut it scared the cub and sent him off bawling while he ran down the riverbank. I could hear the chain of the trap clanking on the rocks as he ran off in the distance. I felt horrified at the thought of him not being able to shed himself of the trap but after thinking about it, I decided it would probably not be a problem as Cowboy did not have much trouble freeing himself and I hope the bear would be able to un-catch himself with little or no problem. I would have liked to see where the trap clamped onto the cub but now I hope the experience will help the bear understand that the lodge is not a safe place for them to be comfortable with.

10/13

It snowed all morning but in the afternoon the clouds cleared so we decided to take the skiff for a ride up lake. Warren warned us to stay by the shoreline with the skiff as the weather could change faster than we could get back to shore. Heavy winds could create monster waves, which could be deadly for us. The water is too cold to swim in and even if we made it to shore somehow, we would be challenged to get back to the lodge safely. With that in mind, we loaded the dogs, rifle, supply backpack, and headed along the shoreline towards the head of the lake. Each bend that we rounded took us into a new world.

As we passed around the large rock formation that can be seen from the lodge we came to the face of sheer rock cliffs, heavy with bird droppings. We bobbed in the water looking at the rocks then our eyes focused in on a nest built on a rock and we saw the gyrfalcon! She had been watching our every move while sitting silently and motionless. The discovery of her nesting place was thrilling as was the fact that she stayed instead of flying away enabling us to get a great look at the magnificent bird. We bobbed in the water watching her while she did not take her eyes off of us. Deciding we had disturbed her long enough, we continued our journey in unspoken amazement as we passed waterfalls, countless eagles, and a total of eight bears along the lake shore lines. As soon as the bears heard the boat motor, they took off running proving these bears understand the sound of a motor meant humans and danger. I find absolute pleasure in watching the mighty creature as they go about daily bear life. It is more than a sight, it is an experience.

We came upon a bright yellow old army camp trailer with big rubber sand dune tires. It is made with metal only having one very small window and the door. Barrels and wood is strapped to the trailer to float it up lake to its current location. We beached the skiff to check it out. It is used as a spike camp for hunters and should be equipped with supplies for survival. It contained a Coleman stove, coffee, canned foods, utensils, and blankets. The small window on the unit has been broken out and birds are getting inside making a mess of the dried goods also leaving lots of evidence that the trailer is a nice place to hang out. The rain is getting in through the broken window and the wool blankets are wet and smelly. We loaded the blankets and empty fuel cans to refill and return on the next trip up. I will feel better knowing that the unit is set up just in case it is needed. When we reached the head of the lake the temperature dropped and got down right cold. Rain began to fall so we headed home. By the time we arrived at the lodge, we were wet, cold, and glad to have a warm and dry place to go inside.

Later this afternoon the dogs started barking so I looked out the dining room window and saw one of the large four cubs by the porch. Instantly I remembered the story Warren shared when his dog jumped from the floor onto the table in front of the same window barking furiously at a bear. Instead of running the bear stood up on his back legs putting his huge paws on the windowpane and began to hit against the glass with his paws while Warren's dog continued to stand his ground on the other side of the glass. Amazingly the window did not break and eventually the bear left. I was very relieved when this bear moved on.

10/14

Today is quiet and sad news came over the radio that Don Johnson is very ill.

Allen and Arlene are preparing for the flight to Kenai as they wish to spend some time with their beloved friend. The news brought out a heavy feeling in my heart and it was though I could feel his presence even stronger now. His dreams, passion, and much of his adult life was spent here at the lodge and he loved this life. Don started building the lodge in the 1950s. I have had the opportunity to experience this adventure because of Don's dreams and hard work. His ingenuity and determination built this fabulous lodge so others can have an experience they will never forget. My heart and prayers go out to him and his family.

The resident fox showed up again today. The fox and Party-girl use to play a game of cat and mouse together but now that Cowboy is here the two dogs chase the fox when the fox comes to the lodge. It is entertaining to watch as the dogs are no match for the speed and wit of a fox. Racing across the tundra the fox darted back and forth until reaching a den in the ground leaving the dogs in fox dust.

10/16

I awoke to bears in the yard and on the porch this morning. Rick had placed some garbage in the adjoining building instead of taking to the dumpsite and burning it and one of the cubs has found it and is interested. I watched as he stood up on his hind legs sniffing and scratching at the window. Seeing the bear stand up about 4 feet from me gave me a sense of how big the cubs are. The cubs are huge. After the bear was gone I went outside to examine the marks. Even as a two year old the cub can reach higher than I can.

This afternoon the sow and four cubs came into the yard during daylight hours, again, which means they are getting much too comfortable here. We felt we had to give them some bad experiences so I stepped out on the porch and sternly demanded that they go away, which did not work. All of them just stood there watching me while I yelled and demanded they leave. My actions eventually provoked them and the largest of the four cubs began curling his lips and clicking his teeth at me. While doing so the bear suddenly made a swift charge at me! I found out that I could also be quite quick because in one move I was back inside the lodge with the door slammed behind me! My heart was thumping and I was shaking as I went to the kitchen window to see if they were leaving or not. The bears had no plans to leave and stayed long enough for us to go get some firecrackers. We lit several and threw them out the window, which also did not seem to faze them, much to our surprise. The next attempt was to shoot bottle rockets at them which did work, but almost too well as one of the rockets shot a cub and got stuck in his fur causing his coat to start smoking. I was terrified to think the bear might be on fire yet relieved to see the bears running down the beach. I watched until they were out of sight and to my delight no flames were spotted.

Rick decided to go out hunting and brought back a fox. I detested the idea but he had his own reasons. He got sick while he was attempting to skin it and I suggested that he leave the rest of the animals alone.

5

Downstream

10/17/94

Today the adventure was in the skiff heading down river. The water remains high enough allowing us to go downstream so we want to take advantage of that and the mild temperatures. We saw a lot of bear, fox, and bird tracks as well as, many eagles while we slowly worked our way down the winding river. I was full of excitement with each bend that we came around, not knowing what to expect. After endless curves we finally came to the shores of the Bearing Sea. We banked the skiff far up river from the mouth of the sea and headed out on foot to explore the abandoned Aleut Village that once existed here. The few buildings still standing are old and beaten by the winds of time, and the bears. One of the remaining buildings is the church. I stepped inside and was pleasantly surprised at the peaceful and calming effect I felt. I tried to imagine what life could have been like living here before the onset of foreign people came and changed life forever. I understand the necessity of change yet in standing here I felt sad. The hard but simple and loving life the natives had known is altered forever.

While we searched around and basked in the past, we noticed clouds forming realizing the need to get started back on the long and slow journey of the meandering river. Forging our way home was very slow as we pushed against the current. We had just passed the spike camp, about half way between the sea and the lodge, when the boat motor started spitting and cutting out. The thought of walking did not bother me but knowing how many bears are out there definitely did. We rode in silence as we slowly crippled our way back up river, bend after bend, until relief over came me rounding the final curve bringing the lodge into sight in the distance. Home sweet home never looked as good as it did right then.

As we approached we heard the buzz of a plane before it came into sight. We had seen and heard this plane earlier while we were in the river alerting us that someone was flying in the area so we definitely felt it important that get back to the lodge. As we approached the dock we watched the tail dragger plane circle the airstrip before landing. The pilot stepped from the plane and walked to the dock waiting for us to arrive in the skiff. He introduced himself as Carl, who had spent the season at a neighboring camp along the Sandy River. I had heard him talk over the radio. Sandy Camp's hunting and fishing season has ended and Carl was busy flying the supplies out and breaking camp. The camp is very primitive. Soft tent camping in this wind and rain, with these bears is not my idea of a relaxing vacation. While Carl was at Port Moller, he noticed the mail for Bear Lake and decided to fly it in to us also gave us the news that Don had passed away. Don was gone, but the memories will remain, forever.

6

Solitude

10/23/94

I decided to go out and pick cranberries, which kept me busy for two days. I cooked them making the most wonderful sauce and canned several jars. The tundra is heavy with cranberries, crowberries, and Labrador Tea. The bears love the berries also. I enjoy the tea and was excited to discover it so I have been picking it to dry as well. I learned about Labrador Tea while living on the Kasilof River. Reading, exploring and fishing was my life at the time.

A new sow and twin cubs were spotted in the area today. She bothers me as she acts very tense and irritable. I sense a bad aura about her and that makes her dangerous. I have not felt this with the other bears. Her cubs are very small and appear fragile. The mother bear had her cubs stay on the lodge side of the river bank while she crossed the river cautiously, sniffing the area, and checking out the other side, then crossed back. Next the sow had the cubs follow her but instead of swimming while she crossed the mama bear stood on her hind legs and walked across the river with her cubs swimming behind her. The movements of her arms swinging appeared human-like. It was creepy. I will avoid her at all costs.

10/24

I went to bed this evening with an uneasy feeling. The dogs and I heard noise outside and when I looked out the window with the flashlight I saw the sow and four cubs. As I looked around with my face pressed against the glass my eyes focused on one of the cubs standing on the porch staring back at me. The moment seemed to last forever as we looked into each other's eyes. I was the one who gave in and shut off the flashlight and when I turned it back on only seconds later, the bear was gone. I did not hear the cub leave.

10/26

Last night brought in fresh snow, which I cannot resist so I bundled up and headed outside as soon as it got light. It is fun to be the one to make tracks in the smooth undisturbed blanket of snow. With the rifle in hand and both dogs at my side I headed up the lake shore, over the ridge and walked the valley behind, ending on the back side of the dump. The snow is deep making each step difficult yet I welcomed the fresh air and the work out it gave me. I spotted the four cubs and sow and because of their routine, I felt confident of where they were heading. Her routine was to walk the overflow waters of the river downstream towards the Fish and Game cabin, cross the river and head up stream on the other side. As I watched, that is exactly what they did. I continued with my journey back towards the lodge only to discover that the new sow with the tiny cubs stood between the lodge and me. Because I am leery of her I was not comfortable with the situation and turned back to find another route discovering, another bear running in the direction from which I had just come. My heart began to race and I thought I could hear the beating of it. The reality of visible bears on three sides of me now and the meanest of all stood between the shelter and I was not a good feeling. I kept the dogs close attempting to divert their attention away from the bears while I sat down in the snow and waited until Ms. Grouchy finally moved on enough that I felt it would be safe to work my way back to the lodge, which I was able to do.

After cooling off and settling down, I went up to the lounge to sit on the deck to see what all the bears are up to. The four cubs and mom are playing across the river. They felt real spunky today and it was especially amusing to watch them run, jump, roll, and dart about. They wrestled with each other and mom even got into to the action at one point. All of a sudden the sow flopped down on the ground rolling and rolling as she scratched her back. Her arms and legs were flying in all directions. One of the cubs went to her, watching curiously, then all of a sudden, the cub flopped down on the ground attempting to copy her. I am sure the patterns in the snow were making snow angels. The snow was really flying. Both bears were covered in white when they stood up. The dogs began to get excited with all the commotion and began barking so the bears went on their way.

10/27

I am still not getting much sleep. Between the dogs barking and Rick staying up all night watching TV life is getting a little crazy. I am trying to start each new day with positive thoughts in mind remind myself to appreciate the wonderful life around me.

Fishing remains good. All salmon and Dolly Varden are released. I decided to go for a walk down stream and discovered something white in a deep hole in the river. After several attempts with a long alder stick I retrieved a walrus skull. Most of the ivory teeth were missing but a few remained so I hauled it back to the lodge proud of the newest treasure to add to the lounge. The cranky sow and little cubs are still hanging in the area. I will be very glad when they move on.

It has continued to snow regularly and we are getting a good ground cover. I have taken the snow machine out several times but cannot get very far. It is confirmed, we are surrounded by water. Some of the backwaters, that cut into the tundra are only a few feet wide yet are five or more feet deep. The tundra is boggy and the grass mounds make traveling of any kind very difficult. The bear sightings are decreasing as the weather worsens. The fishing is starting to slow down now.

7

New Friends

10/28/94

Another resident of Nelson Lagoon, Theo Chesley, flew his Cessna 180 to the lodge today bringing mail, produce, milk, and dog food. Having a visitor is so exciting that it makes me wonder about how simple life has become. The fun of a visitor is always welcomed and mail days are very meaningful. Hearing from family and friends, reading new magazines and catalogs are exciting. It has been three weeks since anyone had flown in to the lodge so there was a lot of outgoing mail. Allen and Arlene are not home from Kenai yet but Theo said he would fly in every couple of weeks to check on us and bring mail and supplies. He did not stay very long due to the ever changing weather conditions and limited hours of daylight. As usual, I stood on the edge of the runway and waved goodbye until I could no longer hear or see the plane.

I have been seeing a single young cub across the river daily now. I cannot help but think something has happened to his mom. The cub does not appear old enough to be on his own and wanders around as though he is lost. Nature will take care of its self. It saddens me though, as I wondered if nature was the reason his mother is not around.

The dog alarm went off around 2 am so I got the flashlight, looked out the kitchen window and spotted some small bear tracks in the fresh snow. I went back to bed but could not sleep so checked out the window again, only to find some large tracks as well. I lay back down again, but for the third time, got up. Now I could hear the bears sniffing and snorting around the building and when I looked out the kitchen window this time I saw the two tiny cubs and scary mom. I definitely do not want these bears getting comfortable around the lodge so I grabbed a pan and wooden spoon, opened the window quietly then began banging and yelling. It did scare the cubs something terrible as they ran off as fast as they could, squealing as they ran, but mom stood her ground and did not run. In fact she stood up to challenge me. I did not back down either. I continued to yell and bang the pan at her. We both stood there, our eyes locked on each other while time seemed to stand still. I was grateful when she finally gave in to her cub's cries and went back down on all four legs running off to catch up with them.

10/29

I finally had a quiet night as far as bear patrol went but a large storm passed through the night and the heavy winds woke me several times. The storm left behind a lot of fresh snow, which has drifted everywhere. I have never seen the side of a building white with snow before today. As I was cooking breakfast I noticed a magpie is trapped in the airplane hangar and was flying against the window attempting to escape. I went out to free her and as she flew out the door she followed me back to the lodge jibber jabbering as I walked. I was not sure if she was thanking me or scolding me but as it turns out she must have been thanking me, since then, she has stayed close to the lodge. She sits outside the door and whenever I come out she follows me. When I go for walks she flies ahead, landing on a branch or rock, then when I get close she flies ahead again. The magpie makes all different kinds of sounds as she goes. I attempt to copy her, but do a poor job of it. She usually answers me anyway. I am trying to get out and walk everyday in an attempt to prevent cabin fever. Today as I sat in the snow on top of Dump Ridge (I've named it) I could not resist the fresh snow and began eating it as though it were a snow cone on a hot day. I know that eating snow is against the rules of survival, but I was close to the lodge. I sat there eating my cone and tried to think of a way to put my sights, thoughts, and feelings down on paper as I was experiencing them. Words cannot come close to what I am feeling. The majesty, tranquility, beautiful vegetation, and wildlife make this desolate place so large and alive and me so small. While I sat there content with life, I watched as a storm from the north worked its way towards me. I decided it was time to head back to the lodge and began my journey but had waited too long as within minutes, the storm was upon me. That is why you do not eat snow.

The cold wind blew intensely against my face and the hammering snow made it very difficult to see. I walked down to the bottom of the ridge to use it for a guide and got into some deep mud, which came up over the top of my boots. It was difficult to get my leg out of the mud and when I finally did free myself; my foot and leg were wet and cold. Typically, that would not be a big deal. Here it can be. It was snowing so hard that I could not see so I climbed back up and over the ridge virtually on my hands and knees to walk the lakeshore in for a guide. The hood on my parka had to be closed so tight that only a very small peek hole remained exposed. On top of it all I came upon fresh bear tracks that turned out to be Ms. Cranky herself and the tiny cubs. I was uneasy with each bend that I rounded but to my relief did not spot them. There is something quite mystical about placing my foot by the tracks of a bear. It was though we connected together in some way. A chance to show each other of our existence and at the same time, accept each other and our territories. I came across some large bones that were strewn about then found one bone that had been urinated on. With the amount of snow that was falling, it was clear that it had been recent and it made the hair stand up on my neck. It was more than just a sight, it was an experience.

Finally I was back in the safety and warmth of the lodge and with a hot cup of tea I began reading a book titled, "The Woman Who Married a Bear." Surprisingly it is quite good and hits home with me.

10/30

We are still getting lot of wind and snow and I still enjoy being the first one out to make new tracks. I saw the single bear cub again today. I Hope he makes it through the winter. I named him Lucky; he is going to need all the luck he can get.

The snow is curling over the banks of the river and I dug out a small cave and gently worked myself inside to lie for a while. It is surprising how I felt warm inside the little snow cave.

The fuel lines keep freezing outside the lodge preventing the diesel from flowing in to the heater and I keep waking up to no heat and a cold room. We will have to do something about that. It takes a long time to heat things back up after they have cooled down into the low forties.

I spend a lot of time thinking about my life these days and reflecting on my past, my family, and friends. It is amazing how clear things become without having outside interference to influence and complicate matters. At times I am quite satisfied and then other times I feel so unaccomplished while my mistakes in life echo through my mind.

10/31

Happy Halloween! The winds have shifted and are blowing from the south off of the Pacific Ocean, which is warming things up and melting the snow rapidly. Today I made a pattern for moccasins and attempted to make a pair for myself. I carved the pumpkin that Theo had brought in and took some food scrapes out for the Maggie, fox, and other birds. Trick or Treat! Mostly they trick me.

By this evening the winds have changed again going from 55 mph to 70 mph blowing from the northwest bringing the temperatures back down. I have been watching the windsock along with conditions, which is teaching me to recognize the different weather patterns. I am also recording the barometric pressure and use this information in dictating how far away from the lodge we should go or if the skiff should be used or not. It is all a reliable source of information. While the winds blew so heavy today I watched as several 55-gallon drums went rolling down the airstrip and out across the tundra. That explains why I have seen miscellaneous items in rather odd places while out exploring.

After the wind settled I went out for a short walk past the dump and noticed that the bears are getting into what is left of the garbage after burning it. Between the bears and the wind a big mess has been made in the area. I picked up an empty can of evaporated milk that had bear teeth marks through it and kept it for a souvenir from a bear. It gives me an odd feeling to hold it in my hand after a bear has had in his jaws.

I walked over to the lakeshore and stepping down off the bank I was delighted to find my first eagle feather! It is so beautiful and in perfect condition. The feather is from a young eagle and has the marbled colors of brown and white. I felt it appropriate as I feel like a young child with all there is to learn out here. I accepted it as a gift from the eagle and will always treasure it. As I walked back to the lodge against the wind and the wet snow that was falling, my parka became so weighted down that it made it more difficult to walk than it already was. By the time I reached the lodge I felt like I was packing a block of cement.

As I crossed the yard I noticed grouchy and the tiny cubs walking along the opposite side of the river. All at once the sow turned and with her paw slapped the tiny cub across his face! Her movements and actions startled me. Again, it was too human-like. I also have no idea what the cub may have done to get slapped, as it did not appear to have done anything. I have a real problem with this bear.

Another thing I have been attempting to learn while passing time is antler carving. I need a lot of practice. I laughed at the results of my first attempt wondering if it was worth the smell that comes along with bone carving. The dust was awful so I decided to get some fresh air and walked down to the Fish and Game cabin for a break. The cabin is built on the banks of Bear River where an overflow or backwater stream joins the river. In the summer a wooden fish weir is placed across Bear River while Fish and Game Management personnel count the fish that pass through the weir. The cabin is only occupied for a short season.

A tower has been built for the workers to sit on while they count fish, as they would not be safe from the bears without it. I climbed the ladder to the top of the tower and the view opened up a whole new world. Eagles perch there frequently and have left a lot of castings. It is exciting to be in the spot where I have seen birds perch for hours on end. I could see for miles and noticed that the backwaters are freezing up. I am glad for that as it will provide access to new places. I stayed on the tower for close to an hour scanning the tundra and hills, but the dogs are nervous when I am up in the tower, so I climbed down and headed back to the lodge.

Looking down at the dogs from the top of the tower

11/2-5

I have been doing a lot of baking. Not only does it give me something to do it also helps warm the place up. It is fun trying new recipes and I am proud to say I have gotten pretty good at baking bread. I like to bake bread twice a week which keeps us with fresh bread and it is so good to eat it warm out of the oven.

Paul, Warren's cousin who lives in Nelson Lagoon called on the radio and told us that Allen and Arlene were coming home but flying in on the commercial airline as the plane Allen flies has issues that need to be repaired. The plane belongs to the lodge and Allen keeps it full time to fly errands for the lodge. Planes are like cars to these people.

I am working on a jigsaw puzzle and while I sat at the table I spotted another new sow and two cubs heading across the tundra towards the lodge. I watched them work their way past the dump, up the hill, and head towards the lake. These cubs are very playful and mom also appeared to be good-natured as she frolicked with cubs. It is delightful watching them so I got the binoculars and followed them until they were no longer in sight. The trio made good time with one mission in mind, a warm place to sleep.

11/6-7

The winds have changed direction again bringing in warm air and melting the snow. I am amazed at how quickly things change around here. I have been spending quite a bit of time antler carving and just when I seemed to be getting the hang of it, the dremel tool burned up bringing an end to that career. The next craft I am attempting to learn is finger weaving. There are several different weaves I have tried and at the moment I am working on a woven bag for my daughter. The biggest problem I am having with weaving is how sore my neck and shoulders get. I have to stop before I want because of the pain. The positive side to that is, it does not consume all my time forcing me to stop then I go outside.

Rick has set up a trap line and since he does not get up until late. I go out, check and spring the traps every morning. He walks the trap line in the evening and so far the only thing that I have found is that the varmints are good at getting the bait without getting caught. Good for them.

Since it has warmed up the snow is slushy and workable so I built a snow bear man today. Rick came out and changed it into a snow bear woman.

11/10

I have been noticing a lot of ptarmigan around the lodge so I went out with the shotgun to try my hand at that. I am surprised that I feel ok about shooting at these birds because I do not like killing animals. I did get a few birds not as many as I expected for shooting into a decent size covey right in front of me. Successfully shooting a flying bird is a lot more difficult than I expected it to be. The feathers are changing color for the winter and even though much of the bird is white, they have beautiful patterns. I saved the feathers for crafts but cannot say much about eating the bird. I have decided that they would make good shoe leather. There is so little meat anyway.

I am still checking traps and only finding sneaky critters. I have been kind of blue lately. I will be turning forty soon and the mistakes that I have made frustrate and embarrass me. I hope that forty years from now I can look back and feel better about my accomplishments. I need to set the past free and learn from it all and move on.

11/11

I woke up this morning to rain and bare ground, except for the snow bear, the snow is gone. I let the dogs out and Cowboy ran straight to the trap that is set behind the dump in a culvert with water flowing through it. Cowboy was barking furiously which told me that something had been caught. I put on my gear and walked out to see what all the fuss was about and was not happy to see that an angry and frightened little mink was in the trap. I tried to find a way to free it but could not get near it without it hissing and franticly fighting to free himself. I did not want to get bit even though I had gloves on and I was unable to help him. This afternoon I went out and removed all of the traps I could find.

We came across an English/German Dictionary and spent two days writing a letter in German to Rick's dad. John speaks fluent German and we thought he would get a kick out of it. It is harder to do than I expected.

Several VCR movies are here so tonight we watched "Fried Green Tomatoes." I really enjoyed the movie but it made me miss my family even more.

11/12

The snow is back again. I am enjoying the fact that I just do not know what to expect next. Cowboy has started a bad habit of sneaking off when I go out to shut off the generator. Several times he came back hours later and it worries me terribly. Last night, he came home with an injured leg and is not walking on it. His leg has a deep gash in it so that has slowed him down. He is taking good care of it and it will heal.

My latest mission has been to make a leather Christmas stocking for my granddaughter, Hailey. I trimmed the top of it with fox fur and beaded her name on it.

Tonight when I walked out in the dark to shut down the generator I felt relaxed and at ease as I have not seen any bear signs for days now.

8

Biding Time

11/14/94

The snow is back again and the moon is full creating enough light to see perfectly at night. The dogs do not sleep much during the full moon as outside of the lodge the animals are moving and busy. The water level of the river is dropping providing access to new and farther places. I walked down stream and found my second eagle feather. What a thrill! My neck and shoulders have really been bothering me so I decided not to weave for a few days. I walked farther up the lake shore than I had been in the past until I came to a patch of slimy rocks which made walking very difficult so turned back. The dogs are always eager to explore and my little magpie buddy is still hanging close to the lodge and going with the dogs and I on our excursions. She chatters the whole way as she flies ahead and waits for us to catch up.

When I returned to the lodge I still did not feel satisfied enough to be inside so I put on chest waders to see if the water was low enough for me to walk across the river. I was surprised to discover how shallow it was as the deepest part only came up past my hips. The dogs swam across and we entered another new part of our world. The first place I headed was to a location where I had seen a bird feeding frenzy going on. Eagles, ravens, magpies, and sea gulls, went wild over something but all I found were bits and pieces of a carcass that has been cleaned and scattered to the point that the animal was not recognizable. I walked across the very rough terrain to the first knob on the hillside where I had seen the sow and four cubs resting many times. There were lots of bear droppings and the grass was smashed down where they laid. I sat down in their bed feeling honored to be in their house. I chuckled as I thought of the story of

"Goldilocks and the Three Bears" but it really would not be too funny if the bears came home and found me in their beds. As I lay there what I felt was not fear, more like enchantment. The dogs were growing restless wanting to move on so we headed farther up the lake shores until the rain began which turned us back. I found one eagle feather but it had been lying on the ground for a long time, I left it as it was. Forging the river again, I was home and as usual, tired, wet, and amazed.

11/15

The wind blew hard and the rain pounded all through the night and the day, keeping us all inside. I worked on a leather pouch that I am making but my hands are getting sore and torn sewing leather without a leather needle. I wrote to Laurie and asked her to send some leather needles to me. The Johnson's are very good to get us whatever we ask for but it can take several weeks, even into months as mail pick-ups and deliveries are sometimes few and far between.

11/16

The dogs woke me up at 4 am so I let them out and as I opened the door there was a fox standing on the porch. The fox lived up to his sly reputation and ditched the dogs abruptly. I watched them as they continued to run around, noses to the ground trying to track him. Silly dogs are no match for the fox.

11/17

It has been quiet for a few days until freezing rain woke me while it hit against the windows. As the day progressed the conditions improved so we launched the skiff and headed up the lake. We rounded Falcon Crest and were a little disappointed that the falcon was not there, but we did see many eagles, which is always a treat. When we glided by, some would fly off while others sat motionless watching us as we passed. I could feel them staring at me.

When we came to military unit spike camp, we beached the skiff and unloaded fuel, dry blankets, and other supplies that we brought to restock the camp. Several wooden shacks had been built in this spot but none withstood the strong winds and determination of the bears. The unit looks terribly out of place but it remains standing.

Bears have been rubbing and chewing on the wood used to float it into its location. They are making a big mess of things. The scratch marks show how far up the bears can reach, much further than I can.

We continued to the head of the lake and beached the skiff to explore. It was very exciting, as we knew that if there were still any bears out, this is most likely where we would find them. It did not seem to slow us down though and in fact it was a big part of the attraction for me. I found two eagle feathers and was astounded at the many bear tracks in the sand. Some tracks were old, but most looked very fresh. I followed the tracks as though I was hypnotized. Many of the tracks were so fresh they clearly showed the patterns of the paws. Some bear prints even showed details of hair on the paw and in between the toes, while the sharp bear claws dig deep in the sand.

We walked up a channel of water following some large moose tracks that were also fresh. All of a sudden something in the water splashed sending me up in the air and my heart into a danger zone. It was a relief to discover that it was a river otter. The otter seemed as curious about us as we were about him. He followed us up stream as we walked he swam under the water popping up in a different location each time. We came to a huge mound of mud, a home built by beavers. It was so well built that I was able to walk on top of the mound without any sign of it giving in. As I stood on it I could smell a very foul odor coming from inside. The occupants started grunting and growling which startled me and for a moment I wondered which of the mighty animals might come busting out of the mound. I decided to leave and scrambled off. In doing so, I discovered a family of otters coming in and out of the mound from under the water. That was that a relief but I was still a bit spooked after that. The alder patches are thick and the skiff was quite a distance away. Even having the rifle with us did not bring me much comfort as we headed back to the beach. At moments like this I wonder why I put myself in these situations. But the otter eased my uncertainties by entertaining us as we walked back to the skiff. The otter followed and frolicked seeming to enjoy showing off and confusing the dogs. Several times he would swim towards us underwater, come up close by, look at us and grunt. The otter's actions were fun and playful.

The air was getting colder and just as we got back on the beach I looked up and saw a single bear standing on his hind legs watching us. The bear was between the skiff and us and once again my heart began to pound. The bear turned out to be a good bear, as he went down on all four paws and ran away.

We rounded the east shores of the lake and spotted another single bear running for the high country in an attempt to get away from us. I felt bad to upset his task. More bears were spotted as we worked our way down the shoreline. The larger bears ran immediately when they heard or spotted us but the younger bears tended to stay longer showing some curiosity in us. They obviously had not had the bad human experience yet.

We arrived back to the safety and warmth of the lodge and I was humble and thankful for my opportunity of real "Northern Exposure".

11/18

Today was a rare day as it was completely windless. The lake was like glass as the sun rose over the mountains around 9:30 am. What an awesome sight. Peace and beauty at its best. Paul radioed that he and Theo wanted to fly in today to deliver mail and supplies. A radio call was always made with us before flying in to check the weather and airstrip conditions. We reported good conditions and excited to have people coming preparations began for visitors. An apple pie was baked and fresh coffee was on the stove and waiting. As soon as I heard the buzz of the plane I went out to welcome our visitors. Theo made three passes before he touched down and I began to get concerned that something was wrong. It turns out something was wrong, but it was not with the plane. One of the young members of the village had taken his life the night before. A pit rose in my stomach as the news was relayed. The three of us unloaded the plane in silence and the two of them were back on their way again. As always, I stayed on the edge of the airstrip until I could no longer see or hear the plane. Even though I had not met the young man, I was deeply saddened and went inside in silence.

Paul had also told us that Allen's plane still was not repaired so Allen and Arlene would not be home for a while. It had been four weeks since anyone had flown in, which felt like a very long time to us and now it was uncertain when the next delivery would be. I am thankful however, that Allen discovered the problem with the plane while still in Kenai instead of up in the air. It makes the mail drops seem rather unimportant. Life in the bush, expect the unexpected.

11/19-20

Again the wind has changed course blowing from the north and dropping the temperatures. It was eighteen degrees out today but with the wind chill it was minus twenty-four. It felt like it too. The oil burner fuel lines are freezing again and I woke up to a whopping forty-two degrees in the room. Something is going to have to be done about this. It is miserable. I have not been getting out much because of rainy conditions so I have been spending most of my time making Christmas presents. I am making all presents this year ranging from leather items, to woven goods, cross stitch angels, and jewelry. It has been fun.

11/21-24

The temperature dropped to eight degrees last night but I went out for a walk anyway. The dogs and magpie followed along. The snow is very crunchy as I step through it and the ice crystals are stunning in the sunlight. I spent most of the day preparing for Thanksgiving tomorrow. A feast for five, Rick, the two dogs, one magpie and myself.

I was working in the kitchen when I heard the pilot from Penn Air announce that he was approaching Nelson Lagoon and had Allen and Arlene on board. That meant that they were not able to bring the plane home with them. It was a disappointment but I was glad that they would be home with their families for the holidays.

The "Wizard of Oz" was on TV tonight and I agree with Dorothy, there is no place like home.

Happy Thanksgiving!

We had a nice day and a great meal but the highlight of the day was talking to our families over the radio with Paul's assistance. He made the call on his phone then after getting our party on the line he would hold the phone receiver to the radio mic, clicking back and forth so we could hear and talk. It was a bit of a struggle but wonderful to hear everyone's voices. It was hard for me to talk without choking up. It felt strange not being with my family and friends for the holiday. This is the first holiday season that we have not been together.

11/25

Warm winds are blowing again and the snow is on a rapid melt down. I have been busy finishing Christmas gifts and packaging them for shipment. The news reported tonight that Fairbanks broke an 85-year-old record plunging to 45 degrees below. Wow! That is really cold for this time of the year.

11/26

I was pleasantly surprised to wake up to snow again this morning with the temperatures holding in the mid-thirties. I was anxious to get outside only to be irritated when I discovered that Rick had set traps again. He had not said anything to me about me removing them. I noticed Parti-girl had not been following any longer so I backtracked in the snow, which led me right to where she was caught in a trap. When she saw me she started squealing. Just like a child. It took several tries to get the trap opened and it did not help that she was biting at my hands as I tried to free her. She came out uninjured except for her pride.

I asked Rick to please close the traps but he ignored me. I would have done it but I do not know where he has set them. I was sure I could find a few and the dogs would help. When I do come across one, I spring it then hide it so at least that one would be one less problem.

I was working on crafts when I heard the Penn Air Pilot announce his arrival in Nelson Lagoon with flowers and the casket, which carried Richard's son, the young man who had taken his life.

How tragic, he was only 16. When there is a death, especially a suicide it is a requirement for the villagers to fly the body to Anchorage for an investigation then the body will be returned for burial. In Nelson Lagoon residents are allowed to bury someone where they choose so most homes have family members in their yards, which are identified by a wooden marker usually of Russian origin.

11/27

Not too much going on lately. It has been cold and I am enjoying my morning routine of starting the generator, making coffee, and going out for walks after it gets light. I love how the snow crunches under my feet and glitters in the sunlight. I decided to get the snow machine out and ran in back and forth on the airstrip attempting to pack the snow in the case a plane might want to come in. Cowboy runs alongside biting at the skies. I scold him but he persists. I think he is trying to protect me and wants me to get off of the machine. Somehow I got the job done without running over him.

11/28

I have still been doing some fishing and continue to catch silver salmon but as always, I release them. At this point the salmon are mushy and terrible looking from spawning and I would not consider eating one. The lake has been calm and the setting sun and puffy clouds reflecting over the water show magnificent shades of pastels. It is exquisite to say the least.

11/29

It has warmed up again and I have been freaking out at the mice in the pantry. The situation has gotten so bad that every time we open the door we hear them scatter. Today I went MAD and pulled everything out of the pantry from the floor level up to the shelves they have been reaching. I cleaned the shelves and items on them and set my own trap. It is a five-gallon bucket with a blob of peanut butter in the bottom of it. I sat it on the floor and I left the room. Within minutes I had a taker in the bucket and as I picked up the bucket the mouse ran around in circles as fast as he could go. Actually they are shrews and are smaller than mice; they have no tails and a strange looking snout. I reached in and picked it up but when it wiggled and squealed so did I, and I threw it back into the bucket.

In the cleaning process I found a mothers ring on the floor and will send it to Laurie hoping that she will know who it belongs to.

9

My Favorite Month

12/1/94

Since I was a young girl the starting of December has always excited me. I enjoy the festivities of Christmas as well as, my birthday falls in December. The season has always been magical for me. This year I will be turning forty. How did that happen so quickly?

I let the dogs out but only Cowboy came back so I got dressed and went outside to follow their tacks. I worry about them falling through ice or meeting up with wolves. The paw prints in the snow led me to yet, another trap, and Parti-girl caught again. This time Parti-girl had an embarrassed expression on her face but she held still and quiet while I worked at releasing her. Freeing her went much smoother that way. I walked the usual sites where traps had been set in the past and did find a few more and to my relief, the only thing caught was Parti-girl. I gathered them and hid them in one of the guestrooms under the bed.

12/2

I had radioed Dailey the day before and asked if we could try calling my family today using the same routine as before with the radio. She did not hesitate and I woke up early this morning with so much excitement that I could not go back to sleep. I radioed at 9:30 am to reach Dailey or Paul but got no response. Just after 10 am Paul radioed back. We called Cherry first and it was so nice to hear her voice. It was also fun to hear about the new things that my granddaughter Hailey is doing. We had only been talking a few minutes and because of a storm the radio connection became real broken making it difficult for us to hear each other so Paul began relaying the conversation for us. In the broken words I did hear

Cherry say that she wished that I would be home for Christmas. It tore at my heart as this was going to be the first Christmas away from my family. Even though they are grown and have kids of their own, it is hard. I miss them. Because of the difficulty of hearing we did not attempt any other calls. The day went on and the wind changed direction again bringing in more snow. The snow helped my spirits.

12/3-4

The cold storm has continued for these past few days and I like it. The highest temperature lately was sixteen degrees and having 55 mph winds has taken the chill factor down to minus twenty below. Paul called on the radio and informed us that Warren made arrangements with Theo to fly Allen over to pick up one of the Super Cubs that are in the hanger. That was good news as it will be nice to have our pilot and friend, Allen, back. Now we will just have to wait for the weather to clear so they can fly.

12/5

Several days had passed before we woke up to a day without wind. With anticipation that the guys might fly in, I prepared for company. Finally in late afternoon we received a radio call inquiring about the conditions here at the lodge. After giving a good report the guys did fly in. Theo took right back off so we helped Allen push the flying dress out of the hanger and observed and assisted Allen's attempts to get the Super Cub running. Allen is very experienced and knew all of the tricks to try so by the time the engine was running I had learned some things as well. The attempts consumed several hours of precious daylight and Allen stated that he would still fly over to Port Moller and pick up our mail and offered that one of us could go along. Because of the lack of daylight hours remaining he could only make one trip saying had he gotten the plane running earlier he would have made two trips getting us both out for a break. Rick and I looked at each other and he offered to let me go. Before he could change his mind I was loaded in the back seat of the Super Cub strapped in, ready to fly.

The flight was outrageous! I enjoyed seeing the country between the lodge and Port Moller, but I was not surprised to see the amount of water that separate the two places. The terrain is very rough. Even though it is only about 15 miles away as the crow flies, any other way to get there would be just about impossible. We spotted several fox and some otter tracks on the frozen ponds but no signs of bigger game. As we circled for the landing I was impressed to see how large and nice the runway is at Port Moller. It is gravel and lines up with the shores of the Bearing Sea. Port Moller originally was a military base built during WWll but has long since been closed for that.

Port Moller

Port Moller is now a fish processing plant owned by a Japanese corporation. Pat, the winter caretaker, stays there alone for the closed season. He also has satellite TV which helps a great deal but two big differences are, he has a phone and because of the size of the airstrip Penn Air flies in every Monday to deliver mail and supplies. He was waiting at the air strip for us to arrive as we had radioed that we were coming and he drove us to the plant. It was fun to meet him face to face as we had spoken on the radio many times for several months but had never met. He gave me a tour of the operation and the facilities are very impressive. There is a house, full time generated electricity, store, warehouse, parts department, commercial dining room, dock and several vehicles and four wheelers which make it possible for him to get out on the beach and explore the area. The facility is large and even though it was silent this time of year I could imagine how alive it must be during the summer fishing season.

I was fascinated at the large pictures that lined the walls of the cafeteria. The wonderful pictures are compiled from years of history and included many pictures of people from Nelson Lagoon. We visited as long as we dared noting that Pat was as anxious for visitors as we were, I get it, but because of the lack of daylight, we needed to fly.

The mail and supplies were loaded, I climbed aboard the Super Cub, Allen took his place in the cockpit and we were off again. As we lifted up into the air we flew out over the rough waters of the Bearing Sea. The water looked very brutal and had a deadly facade to it. Allen turned the plane and followed Bear River back to the lodge. I am envious of Pat being able to get out on the beaches. I could see the advantages of being there, but it did not compare to the beauty of the lodge and its surroundings.

Safely on the ground at the lodge we unloaded the plane and Allen needed to be on his way. As it was, he would probably not get to the village before dark. These small planes do not have radar and need to be on the ground in the dark. We bid our good- bys, I stood along the airstrip and when the plane was out of sight and sound I went in to enjoy the mail.

Fresh coffee beans were sent to us along with several letters and fresh produce. Each letter was opened slowly and savored as they were thoroughly read. I went to bed that evening with the memories of the day floating through my mind.

12/6-7

Frozen fog hung in the area all day creating a very ghostly effect.

I spent the day making Christmas goodies and a dog biscuit wreath. The evening fell with warm winds from the south and rain.

12/8

As soon as the weather permitted Paul used the Super Cub to fly in and pick up our outgoing Christmas packages to be mailed from Nelson Lagoon. I was glad to get them going in hopes that they would arrive in time for Christmas.

12/9

The next several days were stormy with wind gusts in excess of 90 mph! I bundled up and went out for a walk, just to see if I could. The force of the wind is amazing. It pushed me around and seemed to suck the air from my lungs as I tried to breathe. I laughed at how I could lean into the gusts and tilt to extreme degrees. The waves from the lake crashed over the top of the dock.

Being hit with flying objects concerned me, but perhaps not too wise, I enjoyed the experience.

12/10

Several nights now I have been falling asleep around 10 pm only to wake up around 1 am unable to go back to sleep. I get frustrated tossing and turning for hours. Without having the generator running there is not much point in getting up or trying to read so I lay there thinking.

The days have been spent decorating for Christmas. I am surprised at the amount of decorations that are here. Even though there is a small fake Christmas tree I am considering bringing in an alder bush to decorate. Coming from the Northwest I have never had a fake tree and did not really want one now but in the end, the alder idea did not work out so I gave in and hung dried jalapeno peppers, a string of lights, and was pleasantly surprised that I liked it.

12/12

It has been raining and I am keeping my fingers crossed for a white birthday, which is something that I have wished for every year of my life. I thought that being in Alaska I could count on a white birthday but I had a lot to learn about Alaska. The state is huge and the weather conditions depend on where you are.

I went for a walk searching for eagle feathers and found a broken one and a white one. The white one is very fluffy and downy. I caught glimpses of the white downy feather while the wind blew, it was exciting to find.

I also found a fresh mound of dirt with a tunnel leading down into the ground which is of course, a fresh fox den. Another surprising discovery was coming across frost patches in the tundra. The ground is fairly warm and clear of snow but I noticed several areas about the size of a dinner plate where the vegetation was completely white and frosted. I thought that was bizarre.

Pat radioed us to inform us that several packages arrived for us at Port Moller so now we are excited to get them.

I baked bagels today. They turned out pretty good for a first attempt but there must be a trick to it, I will practice as it was fun.

12/13

Dreams do come true. It snowed today! What a special birthday treat. I spent the day eating all kinds of my favorite foods including birthday cupcakes and built a fire in the lounge spending most of the day there. I plan to keep the fire burning for the twelve days of Christmas, which starts today. We lit fireworks this evening shooting them off of the deck. Cowboy chases the fireworks. I could hear fish moving in the water and birds stirring in the night. A couple of people from Nelson Lagoon radioed and wished me happy birthday. It was very touching. I am missing my family and wish they were here. Interesting I do not feel like I wish I was there.

12/14

The last few days have been lazy but nice. It has remained cool and crisp outside preserving the snow. The moon is working its way towards full, which has kept the dogs wakeful at night. At one point I woke up, rolled over and just as I looked out the window I saw a shooting star race across the sky. I tried to stay awake watching for other shooting stars but before I realized it had fallen back to sleep and it was morning. I went out to start the generator this morning but the battery was low and the engine would not turn over. I proceeded to start the portable generator and it would not start either. From there I went up to the lounge to add wood to the fire and the fire had gone out.

After all that I decided to spend the day outside so I fished for a while, catching one silver salmon and losing two. I am surprised that salmon continue to be in the river. When I got tired of that, I went for a long walk following the tracks of a fox. I never spotted the fox but had fun following his footprints. The fox took a lot of extra steps going back and forth.

Ice is forming on the backwaters again. I found out that it was not strong enough to hold my weight meaning, I got wet. The dogs get away with walking on it. The dogs were funny as they played slip and slide. I tried playing with them, which is how I discovered it would not hold my weight. Being on the ice there is not much of a threat as the water is shallow and I was close to the lodge. I was fascinated in seeing all the different ice patterns and formations. The ice is all so individual with beautiful glass looking crystals. I crossed the water and got into some mud again which went over the top of my boots. It stuck me to the ground, which made me fall down. What a mess, and the end of my walk for the day.

12/15

Soaking in the bathtub has been the highlight lately. Still having trouble getting the main generator started.

Rick insists on setting traps so I have been watching where he goes to follow, spring and retrieve them. I found a magpie in one of them today and her leg was broken. I got Rick and she had to be destroyed. He did not like having to destroy the bird so maybe he will stop now. I am hoping anyway.

Temperatures have been staying low hanging around 3 degrees. A slight wind blew today bringing the chill factor down to minus nineteen. The backwaters are frozen enough now that we can get on them without breaking through so I have been playing with the dogs on the ice again. They seem to enjoy it as much as I do. The exercise feels good.

The fuel lines froze again so I woke up to no heat. We worked at thawing them but they would freeze again almost as fast as they were thawed. We received a radio call from Dailey this evening stating my daughter had called and wanted to talk but at the time, Dailey could not reach me on the radio. I was disappointed to have missed her call but she said all was well, she just wanted to chat.

12/16-17

Today when I was out playing on the ice with the dogs I found it very entertaining to throw rocks for them to chase. In some places the ice is very thick and the water seems motionless yet in others the water is flowing under the ice. I can hear the water running and bubbling under the ice. I came across two sets of larger paw prints today. Wolves! They were very close to the lodge. Because of the dogs safety I do not think I like that.

12/18-19

Paul flew in our mail, packages and brought another Nelson Lagoon resident with him. Prebin has stayed at the lodge several seasons while the lodge was closed over the years and Rick enjoyed talking with him about it. It was his turn to fly to Port Moller but because Prebin had a bottle of whiskey with him, Rick chose to stay at the lodge so I flew with Paul to Port Moller. As always, I enjoyed the flight and a chance to make phone calls. It was a nice break to get out but I will admit flying with Paul is a lot different than flying with Allen. He just does not have the same feel for the plane that Allen does and it shows.

12/20-23

It has warmed up into the twenties and has been snowing off and on. I baked bread and answered letters then I walked up the lakeshore and was surprised to find how deep some of the snowdrifts are getting. The ice is also forming on the lake and I was cautiously walking on it. I had a large dagger with me, my idea of protection, so I chopped through the ice and felt better when I discovered that the ice was a couple of inches thick. Nevertheless, I stayed along the edge. I have not seen any animal tracks lately.

Rick was able to get the generator running this morning but it only ran for about an hour then shut down. Now that fuel line is frozen. The oil lines coming into the lodge are also frozen so there is no heat. I have been staying up in the lounge. I have learned to get extra water while the generator is running as when the generator is off the water pump does not run. I figured that out the hard way.

While sitting and staring out the window I noticed white caps at the head of the lake, which means heavy, warm winds, are expected to arrive at the lodge within about an hour, and that was exactly what happened. I fretted all day as the south winds continued to blow. The temperature went from nine degrees to thirty-five in a matter of a couple hours. I am hoping for a white Christmas and this is not looking good. The snow does not seem to be melting as much as it appears to be blowing away. As the wind grew in velocity the powdery snow is sticking is some very peculiar locations like under the eaves of the buildings. Deep snowdrifts are forming. Large thick chunks of ice began to slam against the shores of the lake by the lodge. The strength of a storm has no mercy or match.

12/24

It is now Christmas Eve and the day was wonderful even though the snow is completely melted. It is not looking good for a white Christmas. The afternoon was spent watching football and baking. This evening we read in the Bible together sharing the story of when Jesus was born. The big surprise was when we noticed that it started snowing! The temperature is back down to freezing and it is white out. How exciting! I said a special prayer of thanks.

12/25

Merry Christmas! It snowed most of the night and I arose to a beautiful blanket of fresh snow. The main generator was left on all night not wanting to take the chance of it not running today. It was a special treat to wake up to modern conveniences and the Christmas lights are so beautiful and soothing. The day was enjoyed as several residents radioed from Nelson Lagoon wishing us a Merry Christmas.

Christmas Tree & Maggie

Paul called our families for us so we could talk via the radio. The storm made it difficult but at least we could hear their voices and it gave us the link.

12/26

Cowboy is still going out for his nighttime adventures. I do not like it but he sneaks off. I have tried following his tracks and he is crossing the backwaters and heading across the tundra. I really do not know for sure what his attraction is out there and it concerns me, especially after discovering the wolf tracks.

The day started out with the weather clear and calm and the sun shining against the newly fallen snow is a very beautiful sight. The wind did kick up and has worked its self into a decent storm with gusts as high as mid fifties. The temperature is holding at thirty-two degrees. It has been interesting to watch for the conditions to change and recognize the changes coming.

Today I could see the snow whisping at the tops of the mountains at the head of the lake meaning a storm would be upon us within a few hours. This is very valuable information in the case that we might be planning an outing, especially a boat ride. The wind arrived at the lodge an hour and a half after I first noticed it. We watched it as it came towards us across the lake. By this evening, it was snowing and blowing to the point of a white out. We both went out to shut off the generator and it was quite an experience, as we had no visibility and struggled to walk against the wind. We came inside with a whole new understanding about how easy it could be to get turned around and lost in a storm.

12/27

The wind got right with it through the night, with gusts up to 85 mph. The snow is still falling and it is wet and heavy. It clogged up the satellite dish causing us to lose the signal. Things get real quiet around here without the TV. Completely losing the link to the outside world is a strange feeling.

The generator would not start and in working with it Rick discovered that the slushy snow had filled the exhaust pipe, which in turn, filled the generator with water. It had to be taken apart and dried it out. It is a whole different world around here without electricity. The dead quiet is almost haunting.

12/28

We woke up to the surprise of a snowfall during the night and again, continue to be amazed how the weather changes so fast and often here. I spent most of the day grooming Parti-girl, as she is full of dread locks. The snow sticks to them making little snowballs that tinkle with every move that she makes.

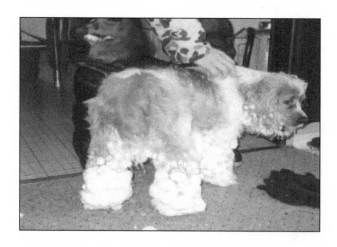

She only stays patient for so long then makes funny growling noises at me.

12/29-30

The following day was nice and for once we were discussing our options for the day when we heard a radio call from Paul to Pat stating that he was flying to Port Moller. That meant he would probably be flying into the lodge as well so we prepared for company. About 40 minutes later Paul radioed us inquiring of the conditions here at the lodge and stating he would be flying in.

This time Rick flew with Paul over to Port Moller, which was his first trip out of the lodge. It was nice for him to get out, meet Pat and see the country between here and Port Moller. It was also the first time that I had been left alone at the lodge and in the silence of being isolated all kinds of things started running through my mind.

Even though we had basically been living separate lives, it felt different now that no one was here but me. Finally I heard the buzz of the Super Cub and I went out to the airstrip to watch them land. They touched down nicely but lost one of the brakes, which sent the plane into the alders before coming to a halt. Fortunately no one was hurt and the plane suffered some damage. A hole was punctured in the fabric. It was exciting for us all but the kind of excitement that we really do not need. After the fact, we learned that Paul had known the brake was bad, which was the reason that Allen had not been flying it. Learning that fact, I felt it showed very poor judgment on Paul's part.

We pushed the plane into the hanger and he worked on the brake, making necessary repairs so that the incident would not happen again. Now the fun of opening letters, packages, and Christmas cards begins.

12/31

New Years Eve has arrived and it is stormy out today. We had gusts up to eighty-four mph. Again I went out for a walk and even though it might not be very smart, I enjoyed the sensation and sights. Many times I would have to firmly plant my feet and try to hold steady to keep from being knocked down. I laughed to myself thinking if I did fall down and began rolling I might not stop until reaching the Bearing Sea.

I was soaking wet when I came inside as the rain gear I had on did very little to protect me. Wind blew the rain up under the layers of clothing and I was thankful to have a dry place to go into. After a nice hot bath and cup of tea we played dice and poker while waiting for the New Year to roll in. Because of the satellite TV we were able and counted down the New Year four times with the different time zones in the United States. When it was really our turn we went out onto the deck and shot off fireworks to celebrate.

10

A New Year

1/1/95

As we were spending a very lazy day watching football and eating snacks we heard the buzz of a plane so I went out just in time to see Theo circle and land. He brought John Jr. with him. They just flew over to wish us a Happy New Year and out for a flight. What a nice surprise and fun to meet another resident of Nelson Lagoon. I tried to feed them and think of any excuse I could muster up to keep them here long as possible. They stayed as long as they dared but due to the fading daylight, they had to be on their way. As always, I stood on the edge of the runway and watched as the plane taxied and lifted up into the air. The plane circled giving me the wing wave then they flew off into the horizon. When I could no longer hear or see them I headed inside once again. Rick and I played cards and it was something different to do.

1/2

Cowboy was restless and disturbed me all night. Rick is still sleeping upstairs most of the time and I am feeling alone. I have made the discovery that out here, alone, really means alone. I took down the Christmas decorations and started a jigsaw puzzle. I have had several days of laziness with the big excitement being, I asked Rick to help me push the Super Cub out of the hanger, so I could sit in it. I wanted to study the instruments and get a feel for it. It took me back to my younger years when I drove so many miles behind the wheel of a parked car. Now I have graduated to planes. It felt good and I could picture myself flying the plane and flowing through the sky. It was tempting to try and start the engine and just drive it up and down the air strip, but I fought the urge and when my brain started working again, I was glad that the plane was not running.

1/3

It has been raining lately so of course the snow is melting again. Even with the bad weather I have been going outside every day. I have not found any feathers lately but I did come across another fresh fox den. The fox really get around constantly making new dens. I am curious if some of them are tunnels.

1/4

Today Dailey radioed that Laurie called and is working to get airline tickets for me to fly home and see my family in the spring. This is exciting for me and it gives me something to look forward to. I have not seen any of my family or friends since coming to Alaska. My two grandkids are young and change so fast during this time of their lives. I am anxious to see everyone.

It sprinkled a little this evening but did not stop us from going for a short walk. We found one small eagle feather, which I always treasure. It was disappointing to see how the ice has melted on the backwaters. Only the thickest chunks remain and the waters are high and flowing fast.

1/5

As we sat watching football playoffs we were surprised to hear the buzz of a plane as Paul landed the super cub. This time along with our mail and supplies he brought another person from Nelson Lagoon with him; Justine Gunderson, who is Theo's mother. It is fun to meet the people that I hear or talk to over the radio. So far, no one has looked like I pictured them.

1/6

The moon is large and the dogs are restless. It is surprising how difficult it is to get a good night sleep around here. Falling asleep late I did not wake up this morning until 9 am, which is late for me. It was a treat to go out and start the generator without using a flashlight. We are gaining daylight hours, and spring will be here in a few months.

While eating breakfast we discussed going for a boat ride as it was calm and clear, but as we spoke the weather changed without warning. The sky from the north darkened and the temperature dropped to 26 degrees, down from 40 degrees within minutes. Everything began to frost before our eyes. Frozen fog rolled in and was so thick that you could see barely see your feet. I was glad that we did not go out and get caught in this storm. Plan B went into effect; I decided to start the job of painting the pantry. The shelves have never been painted and it is taking several coats of paint. I could not find a brush or roller so I am using a sponge to paint with. The fumes were strong and the fog had lifted so we decided to be brave or stupid and launched the skiff into the water.

This time we started out on the far side of the lake and the first thing we saw were three very large moose. It was a real delight, and the first sign of life that we had seen in quite some time. Going farther up the lake we came to a creek that we have wanted to walk up so we beached the skiff and set out to explore. There were a lot of eagle tracks and bloodstains on the ground where the birds fed on salmon. Farther up the creek many other tracks were discovered which included moose, fox, bear, and wolf. I was surprised to discover how large the wolf tracks when I laid my hand beside the wolf paw print to compare.

We cautiously worked our way into the alders. It was very thrilling. Every time that we have come by here in the skiff we had seen bears which made walking very exciting. Even without leaves, the alder bushes are thick and you can only see a few feet around you. Rick began to feel concerned that he had not secured the skiff well enough so he decided to go back and check it to be sure. He handed me the rifle and headed back to the shore while I ventured ahead. Not long after he had been gone the dogs went ballistic barking and carrying on. The adrenaline started pumping through my veins as I put a shell in the chamber of the rifle and removed the safety. I worked myself closer in the direction that the commotion was coming from with the anticipation of seeing a bear or a wolf. I was concerned for the dogs, which kept me going. A short distance from the barking I still could not see what all the fuss was about, so I worked my way closer. I could see something brown that the dogs had cornered and as I got near them I was relieved to see that it was only a porcupine. I was even more relieved to see that neither of the dogs had quills in them. I called the dogs off and we headed back towards the skiff. Rick heard all the commotion and was rushing to get to us. As I explained what the situation was his expression changed from concern to anger and he began to scold me for going into the alders. "Why did you do that?" he grumbled, but before I could answer the look in his eyes showed me that he understood. I did it because I had to. We walked farther up the creek as a light snow began to fall turning us back. On the return trip visibility was poor. We could not see the lodge until we were directly across from it. The sight of the buildings is always so comforting after an excursion.

1/7

Another frozen fog passed during the night leaving everything white and frozen this morning. Nothing escapes as the crystal forms individually on each blade of grass and any items that are exposed.

After putting a second coat of paint on the pantry shelves, we took off in the skiff to get away from the fumes that permeated the lodge. The lake was calm appearing of glass while the sun reflected against the water. I felt guilty disturbing the stillness of it all. We decided to go to Falcon Crest and explore thinking we could not get ourselves into too much trouble as it was fairly close to the lodge. As we rounded the rock we were disappointed to see the falcon perch empty but thrilled at the large number of eagles that sat on the cliffs watching our every move. At times it felt much like Alfred Hitchcock's movie, "The Birds".

The ice formations on the rock wall are mesmerizing. There were waterfalls that had frozen in mid-drop.

We beached the skiff and while we were standing on the shore, we spotted a cow moose with twin calves standing on the ridge above us. I did not want Cowboy to chase them so we whistled and yelled while waving our arms, hoping to persuade them to move on but instead, their curiosity only brought them closer. That could mean two things, she is just curious or she is threatening. The moose continued to watch us as we worked our way up the cliff and allowed us to get pretty close before deciding to move on. It surprised us, as they did not go far, seeming to wait for us to catch up. A moose trick I wondered? We continued to climb and kept seeing them until one point when they were gone, so was Cowboy. I knew exactly what had happened and as I stood there scanning the countryside I saw the three moose running into the next valley with Cowboy right behind them. Bad dog! They were so far away that he looked about the size of a rabbit as he ran at top speed in an attempt to send them to

Russia. Rick whistled and to my surprise, Cowboy heard the call and turned back. I watched him work his way up to us and when he arrived he was panting and very overheated. I sat down on the face of the cliff for quite some time, taking advantage of the spectacular view and allowing him to cool down. The mountains were reflecting over the lake and the sight is one I will never forget.

Working our way up to the top was hard work at times it was very steep and others we had to break our way through the alders. We rose to the top of the rocks above the falcon nest and just sat engrossed in the surroundings. There is a small lake or pond back behind the knob. It appears to be frozen. The view was astonishing and I felt like I was on top of the world. You could see for miles in all directions and looking out over the water is incredibly peaceful.

Noticing the time, we realized that we needed to start back down enjoying the decent much better than the ascent. We came to a steep spot on the hillside and I sat down and slid in the mud and snow, laughing as I leaned from side to side attempting to control myself, while I sped past alders and rocks. Needless to say, I beat Rick down the hill.

Back at the skiff we loaded up, and headed towards home. Cowboy's ears were flying straight up from the wind and it looked so funny. I reached in the pocket of my parka to get the camera and take a picture of him only to find an empty pocket. The camera was gone. With a lump in my throat I told Rick that we had to go back and why. He did not want to turn back stating that it would be like finding a needle in a haystack and reminded me that we were pushing daylight, but he also has grown to know my persistence, so gave in and turned the skiff heading back to the crest. Beached again, he stayed in the skiff as I headed back to the hill where I had slid down while keeping my fingers crossed that I would find the camera there. I was dreading the thought of climbing to the top again but knew that I would if necessary.

It was harder than I expected to even find the exact spot that I descended from but I kept searching for my tracks and finally found a boot print in a patch of snow. I followed the path up and to my delight spotted the camera laying on the ground about half way down my slide. I yelled down to Rick holding up the camera for him to see then began my climb down the hill this time, upright. Back in the skiff again and pushed away from the shore Rick was having a difficult time getting the boat motor to go into gear. Then the shift lever broke off. We bobbed about in the water while he worked with the motor until he figured out how to get it into gear and we were on our way home once again.

Moments like this are very humbling as they make the lodge feel so far away. It felt good to pull up to the dock and unload.

11

Ice

1/10/95

The last few days have been calm, cool and the new surprise was the discovery that the lake is frozen. We went for a walk up the lakeshore and had fun throwing rocks across the ice while the dogs chased them. The rocks made a real unusual sound as they skidded across the ice. It sounded kind of metallic if that makes sense. We played on the ice ourselves, skidding and falling at times, always staying close to shore. In several spots the ice did crack under our feet sending my heart up into my throat, but never did break through.

At one point, we heard an ice crack in the distance; we froze in our tracks while listening as the crack traveled. It kept coming closer and it split right between my legs. It was wild! We walked up the lakeshore until we passed the point of ice and were back to open waters. From there we headed up the hillside and walked a ways farther. You can see both sides of the valleys from the top of the hill, allowing a fabulous view of the lake on one side and the never-ending basin on the other. No animals were spotted but we did find wolf tracks. The wind kicked up from the south so we turned back. As it grew stronger, it began breaking the ice on the lake.

Home again, we sat on the deck watching and listening to the sounds of crushing ice. It is difficult to describe the sound of raw power but from the distance you could hear a roar; much like the sound of a locomotive. As the ice cracked across the lake it had a twang to it and was very outer space sounding. Many times it reminded me of the sounds from the movie, "Star Wars." As the evening moved in we could see large chunks of ice moving in the light of the moon while they broke into smaller pieces. It was daunting to think that just hours before we were out playing on the ice that was now breaking into a million pieces and being pushed around with massive force. I placed a tape recorder on the deck in an attempt to record the sounds, but the wind was mostly all that could be heard.

1/11-13

The wind has continued to blow hard with steady gusts into the 60-mph range. The ice in the lake is completely broken up and is trying to work its way down the stream, but has jammed up and backed into the lake for as far as I can see down the river. The ice is clear and resembles broken glass this time.

Broken lake ice

I walked the river's edge down to the Fish and Game cabin and climbed the lookout tower. Ice is jammed for miles downstream and in the lake where the ice line begins the wind is churning waves of ice creating a thunderous sound.

Bear River jammed with ice

1/14

I am still painting in the pantry and getting outside in the afternoon to escape the fumes.

Today as we walked down stream we came to an open channel where the water has allowed the ice to flow out to sea. The wind is blowing hard enough to cause white caps in the lake. As the waves crest the ice is being tossed upon the frozen layer building it up. The channel continues to open wider which will eventually carry all the ice away.

1/15

A fresh layer of snow fell last night so I got the snow machine out and enjoyed riding it around. The good news for the day is that the pantry is almost finished. The bad news of the day is that something has gone wrong with the satellite receiver and it is no longer working. The TV reception along with our link to the outside world is gone. Now it is really quiet here.

1/17

I have been trying to keep busy with crafts, reading, and writing letters, but I have to admit without the TV the isolation is starting to get to me and it has only been two days. We have been seeing a few ptarmigan but that is about all for wildlife. Life has been pretty still. A large storm passed dumping about 16 inches of snow. It is fun to get out in the fresh snow and the dogs enjoy it as well. They jump and run while occasionally sticking their heads down in the snow looking funny when they come up.

Parti-girl and Cowboy

1/20

Paul and Dailey tried to fly our mail and supplies in but got into an ice storm in the air and had to spend the night in Port Moller with Pat. The ice was building up on the plane in the air so they were grounded while waiting out the storm. Late the following afternoon,

Paul flew in with our delivery and flew Rick over to make some phone calls.

1/23

It has cleared off and I am enjoying the millions of stars in the sky. The temperature has been hanging around 5 degrees and I love the crispness and the way the snow crunches under my footsteps. Allen radioed that he was flying in as Paul left some of our supplies behind, our liquid boxed milk and eggs.

When Allen arrived he had a very interesting passenger with him who is a journalist from Norway named Lars Monson. Lars writes for a sports magazine in Norway. The magazine sends him on outings, and he writes about them. His current project is to walk Alaska. It will take a year to complete and his partner on this adventure is a woman. Allen is flying Lars over the route that they will be walking once they leave Nelson Lagoon. They will come to Bear Lake so it is exciting for us as well. In the short time that we visited Lars appeared to be an interesting and witty person, so we are looking forward to having them for guests.

Lars figures it will take 7-10 days to get from Nelson Lagoon to the lodge. After Allen and Lars left the bright and sunny day was tugging at me so I went out for a very long walk up the beach. The ice is forming in the lake again. As I struggled to cross the rough terrain I could not imagine what it would be like to walk from Nelson Lagoon, and they are walking the entire state.

1/24-26

It is continuing to stay cold and when the wind blows which is most of the time, the chill factor is hanging around minus twenty. You really feel it when you are outside. I started the generator this morning but did not have any running water. It obviously is frozen somewhere so that is the next challenge to face. Most of the day was spent trying to get the water flowing with no avail, and the following day brought the wind chill down to forty below. It is very cold and hard to be outside to work on pipes for more than a few minutes at a time. We took turns. I broke a hole through the ice in the lake and dipped water with a five-gallon bucket to flush the toilet and we are boiling it to use for consumption. I have a great admiration and respect for the strength and ingenuity of the people who have lived life without modern conveniences.

1/27

The water pipes are still frozen. We worked all afternoon to get them running with no success.

1/28

Today Rick took the pipes apart down in the basement where the water comes in and he finally got the water flowing again but now something is wrong with the water pump, it will not build up enough pressure to shut off. When we need water we turn the pump on then shut it off manually. Even though that is a pain, it is great to have the water. It felt like I washed dishes for hours.

The temperature warmed up into the teens and it is snowing again. It was unbelievable to watch two moose and four fox cross the lake on the ice. I was amazed the moose were able to cross without breaking through.

I set the cassette player back out on the deck and played animal call tapes to the fox and laughed as they turned their heads from side to side listening. One of the fox that I have been seeing daily across the lake is a cross-fox. They are called that because of their marbled markings. I had their attention but they stayed away.

12

Foxy Animals

1/29/95

I sat up in the lounge watching it get light this morning and as the sun came up I noticed the three moose browsing across the river. I also saw the cross-fox again. His fur is very pretty with the calico colors throughout his coat. He has been hanging out in the same area that the family of bears slept in so often. Later in the afternoon I went for a walk up the lake and the ice is thick again. I sat on a rock for quite awhile watching an eagle fight with several ravens as they fought over an expired duck. The feathers blew across the lake and a few blew right at me.

The days have been pretty quiet. I have been expecting Rick to say something about the missing traps but he has not so far which I am happy about.

1/30

It has been beautiful out lately. I love the bright sun as it shines on the fresh snow. Everything is so clean and peaceful. The little cross fox is still hanging in the area and I am still playing tapes for him. He is very curious.

I took the spotting scope out on the deck and located three other moose on this side of the lake. The heavy snow must be pushing them down this far. The big excitement of the day was spotting a pair of falcons! I first saw them on the ground feeding and watched them until they headed back up the lake. It is really awesome watching them climb so high in the air, hang there, and then dive swiftly as they made their attack. The "not so bright" ptarmigan did not stand a chance against them. Nature takes its course right before my eyes. I continued scanning the countryside and noticed a couple sets of tracks at a high elevation on the mountainside in a very steep area. There is a smaller set of different looking tracks that follow behind them. I am stumped by what would be up so high.

After the generator was turned off for the day the night fell upon us we took the scope back out on the deck to look at the stars. There are millions of them shining bright tonight and the brightest one showed the colors of the rainbow through the scope. It was exquisite. I really enjoy the quiet when the generator is not running. All I can hear are the sounds of water and the birds. The peace is like nothing I have ever experienced.

I spoke with Pat this evening and he said that he had traveled the beach with the 4-wheeler and the ice chunks lying on the shore are as big as dump trucks. It really amazes me to discover salt water freezes.

1/31

Lazy days. The same fox stays in the same place every day now. He must be busy hunting at night as he sleeps all day. He only gets up to yawn; stretch, circle and curl back up. What a life, much like mine. The three moose across the lake are hanging in the area as well. They must be finding what they need to eat. We took the snow machine out and rode the edge of the lake around the face of Falcon Crest and it was pretty scary and extremely stupid as the water is very deep there. I will not do that again; the fear in my stomach was a deep ache as I held my breath. The entire lake appears to be frozen which everyone says is rare.

As I looked around savoring everything, one of the falcons flew right over us. I could see his eyes watching us as he flew past. He also stirred up a large covey of ptarmigan. They are completely white now and there had to be several hundred of them. We would not have even seen them had they not been sent into flight by the falcon. The trip home went fast even with two exhausted dogs riding on the snow machine with us. We were all glad to be back in the safety of our shelter.

2/1

It has warmed up recently and the snow and ice are rapidly melting again. The temperature today rose to 46 degrees and it rained most of the day.

I stayed inside baking bread and sitting in the lounge watching a standard colored red fox cross on the ice and walk up the hill to the cross-fox.

The cross-fox sat watching the approaching fox with his mouth wide opened and his ears flattened back. When the red fox was close, the cross-fox snapped at the red fox which immediately put its tail between its legs then they both curled up together and went to sleep. Interesting behavior I thought.

The three moose have moved farther down the lake now. Pat radioed to inquire if we had felt the earthquake that hit Port Moller, but we had not. It was very windy today.

13

Blues

2/2/95

The wind and rain has continued and I am feeling pretty blue these days. I have not gone out much due to the weather and I am sure that is not helping. I feel so alone and have been having strange dreams again. Last night I dreamt that I had been shot in the neck. The dreams disturb me throughout the day. I sure hope that I am not coming down with Steven Kings, "Shinning" syndrome.

This evening the snow has started falling again but with no accumulation. When we went out together to shut the generator off and we could barely walk on the ice. Every step was a huge effort to keep from falling as water is standing on top of the ice.

2/3

The weather has improved and today I took a three-hour walk with the dogs. It felt good but the rifle got heavy and was hurting my shoulders. I know it is necessary but I do not like carrying it. I walked up dump hill and continued for several knobs. The walking is very difficult with uneven and constant grass mounds causing each step to jam my hips. I followed some moose tracks then was excited to come across wolf prints, which were also following the moose. I was surprised that it was enticing because the tracks were fresh. As I followed, I became spooked when I came across fresh bones from a large animal. There was still meat on the bones and the dogs were sniffing and tracking the prints. It made the hair on the back of my neck stand up. All of a sudden Parti-girl began barking and took off running with her nose to the ground so I found the highest spot that I could find and scanned the countryside looking for animals or

Norwegians but saw nothing except for beautiful country. On my return to the lodge, I walked on the ice on the lake.

The ice is breaking again and as always, I stayed close to the shore. Each step I took the ice would crack under me and for quite some time I stayed on top but then it happened. With little warning the ice broke under my feet and I was in water up to my hips. The sudden jolt hurt my neck and shoulder but I was thankful the situation was not worse. I felt a bit sheepish and thought I got what I deserved.

It was pretty cold walking from then on as I made my way back to the lodge. To try and stay warm I made a game of running and jumping from ice chunk to ice chunk. Even though the pieces would break and begin to sink under my weight they held me long enough to get to the next piece if I was quick. It also mentally helped me to focus on something other than how cold I was.

At times I purposely challenged small chunks of ice just to see what I could get away with. Needless to say, I was plenty glad to be back at the lodge and after a hot bath and a cup of tea I was as good as new.

2/4

Today was just not a good day. I did not feel good. Babies got the blues. I am board, cranky, and spent most of the day up in the lounge until I accepted a challenge to play a game of scrabble with Rick which was a big mistake. He knows way too many big words for me and every time I built a pitiful word and earned only a few points; he would add a couple of letters to my word and get big points. I got mad over it and told him to stop using my words and make his own. He only laughed and continued to do it so I quit. Not only did I quit but I flicked the board and the letters went flying. That made him mad and he stated that he would never play a game with me again. The situation did not help my emotions so I went up to the lounge and had a good cry.

Spotting the falcon across the river saved today. I continued to watch him as he successfully hunted and ate his prey. He was close enough that I could see the beautiful patterns of his feathers. What a magnificent bird.

I have not slept well the last few nights and I am still having a hard time shaking my poor mood. It was helpful to see new snow, but it upset me further when Rick would not even stay in the same room that I was in. A few hours later, while I was sitting in the lounge I spotted him out on the tundra. He had taken off without saying a word. We know that is risky because if anything happened, I would not have the slightest idea where to go look. The mood I am in I doubted that I would go look for him anyway. I always told him where I was heading when I went out alone and if we left together, we would leave a note on the table stating where we had gone in the case we did not make it back. Paul radioed that he was flying in and I knew that would help my mood but he never showed up, or radioed to say that he was not coming. What is up with these people? Later in the day, I listened to the marine radio as conversations were being held with the Norwegians and several different people in Nelson Lagoon. They had made it to Herendeen Bay and were having some sort of trouble. The reception was broken most of the time so I was only catching bits and pieces. It sounded like someone was going to fly over and pick them up. I said a special prayer for them hoping that they are both all right.

I watched an eagle struggle with a fish in the river. He held it tight with his talons and was not about to let go but was fighting to get it to shore as the fish was too heavy for him. I found it was very interesting the way he was using his wings to paddle in the water. At first it looked as though he was injured. The movements were very awkward as his wings flapped over and forward while he was determined not to let go of his meal. I was glad for him when he finally reached the shore and felt that he really deserved that dinner.

14

Alive Once More

2/6/95

Today was a lot better and moods have improved for both of us. I am thankful for that.

Paul radioed and stated that he had picked up Marit, the female in the Norwegian party but that Lars had continued walking the journey alone. The plan was for her to stay in Nelson Lagoon for a few days then Paul would fly her into the ledge where she would meet back up with Lars.

It has snowed a lot so we took the snow machine out and tied a snow shovel to it with a long rope. We took turns giving each other rides in the shovel as we ran back and forth on the airstrip to beat down the snow. Strange what ideas a person comes up with when resources are limited. It was the most that I had laughed in a very long time.

Cowboy did not think it was as funny and ran alongside me pulling and tugging at my clothes in an attempt to get me off of the shovel.

At one point while I was pulling Rick, the ornery streak came out in me and without warning I headed out across the tundra with him in tow. It was not long before he fell off and stood up covered in snow. I considered the fact that I might be better off continuing in the direction I was pointed and not stopping but he was laughing so I turned back.

15

Norwegian Wanderers

1/29/95

The next day was a bittersweet day for me. Paul did fly Marit in along with mail and supplies and it was exciting to have the company but in the mail came the sad news that my precious Labrador of thirteen years had died. I knew the trip to Alaska would be too hard on her at her age so I had left her in good hands where she was comfortable. Realizing that I would probably never see her again, I said my goodbyes to her when I left Oregon. It was very difficult for me to leave her but not as difficult as it was for me now as this news had come in that she was gone. We had gotten her as a pup when my kids were young and she was every bit as much of a member of the family as the kids are. I am hurting so bad and glad to have company right now. Paul flew Marit in, she is a pure delight.

Then Paul made a second trip to Herendeen bay to pick up Merits' things and upon landing there he discovered Lars waiting. Lars had tried to go on but the terrain had gotten too rough requiring him to turn back. We were all surprised when the Cub landed back at the lodge a second time with Lars on board. The plane was loaded, including the dog sled, which was strapped to the outside of the aircraft. The evening was very nice as we stayed up until morning exchanging facts about our countries and customs. Lars and Marit plan to stay a couple of days then they will walk on from here.

The time is filled with conversation, laughs and lots of food. Lars and Marit are wonderful people and I am enjoying their company immensely. Marit commented on my moccasins so I surprised her by making her a pair. Both of them are pretty tired and sleep later than I do so I worked on them in the mornings without her knowing about it. It was a fun surprise. Lars liked them so much that he offered to pay me to make a pair for him also. I was happy to do that and would not consider being paid for them. The fact that they are here and I have new friends is payment enough for me. Lars is fascinated about the history of Bear Lake and we spend a great deal of time talking about it. Lars takes a lot of pictures and writes every night. The trek that they are taking across Alaska will take a full year. He sends his film and writings home to the magazine in Norway, which prints the ongoing story in the monthly issues. He has also written books and intends to write one about this adventure.

Lars and Marit

Marit and I go for long walks and talk constantly while the guys spend a lot of time playing chess and talking constantly.

Marit and I returning from a walk

They have to travel as light as possible so all they eat while they are out walking is instant potatoes, candy bars, fish, and berries that they can get along the way. When they come to a village or city, in this case the lodge, they are hungry and tired and try to catch up on both.

Marit wanted to bake a cake; it was interesting that I had to translate the measurements for her, as she is use to their method of metric. She had no idea how to use our measurement system, just as I would be equally lost attempting to use theirs. We laugh and really enjoy each other's company. It will be hard to see them go.

1/30

It took an entire afternoon out on the deck, for Lars and Marit to go through their belongings, air out and dry to re-pack for departure. It was interesting to see what they were carrying. Most clothing is wool or some water proof material.

The plans for departure were delayed a day as the weather was too stormy, much to my delight they decided to see what the next day held. I was glad for the extra time with them.

Lars Monsen & Toini

Marit Holm

1/31

    We woke to calm weather and we all knew that today our new friends would leave. It was the most quiet we had been since their arrival. They loaded up and along with their sled dog, Toini; they set out to continue their journey. We walked with them for a short distance then we said goodbye. I was thinking that I will never forget them, as they walked away. I stood and watched, Marit turned and waved and they were gone.

16

Alone Again

2/1-2/95

I woke up today to a fantastic day. I sat on the deck most of the day just feeling the warmth of the sun and listening to the sounds around me. It really amazes me how much of nature that I can hear without people sounds to interfere. It is very relaxing and healing.

The ice on the lake is slowly breaking up and huge mounds of ice are building up on the shoreline. Some of the millions of pieces are very large and in places the ice mounds are around five feet in height. The ice pieces appear to crawl on top of each other on the shore. The movements are subtle but not the sounds as the ice grinds. It moans and groans with each movement.

I am getting excited about my trip to Oregon to see my family and friends. It is only about two months away now and I am feeling restless.

2/4-7

The last few days have been so foggy that you could actually feel the fog. I hope the Norwegian wanderers are faring well. All of the snow is gone at ground level and most of the ice is out of the lake. I went for a walk and found two eagle feathers.

The moon is full again so I have been sleeping upstairs in the spare room as it is darker and keeps the dogs quieter. I am reading books like they are going out of style and do not miss TV at all. I still try to get out and go for walks every day. The only treasures that I have found lately are the peace and beauty that surround me.

I woke up in the middle of the night to Cowboy throwing up a huge pile of gross stinky rotten salmon. Then of course, I threw up trying to clean up the mess. I cannot figure out why dogs eat some of the disgusting stuff that they eat. The fish has not set well with him and he is drinking a lot of water so I am hoping he will be ok. Salmonella is not much of a concern up here and many of the people feed their dog raw fish. I still would not from choice. As a child, I had a dog die from eating raw salmon in the Northwest and I would not take the chance but cannot control what he gets into on his own.

2/8

The next surprise came today when two new faces flew the super cub into the lodge. Gunner, who is Arlene's brother, and lives in Nelson Lagoon, along with a man named Peter Faust who lives in Anchorage, came in for a visit. They brought our mail and as always, it was great to have company and get the outgoing mail sent. We all enjoyed visiting and they did not seem in any hurry to leave so we drank coffee and ate baked goodies as we swapped tales and history of the area.

They both had a lot of information to share and told us that most members of Nelson Lagoon are very superstitious about the lodge and believe that it is haunted. There are lots of ghost stories and most of the natives will not spend the night here. They feel that trouble comes from disrespectful killing and mounting of the animals that are taken for sport here.

The human skull in the rafters of the lounge is also a big concern to the natives. I have to admit I agree with them on that. Gunner said the skull came from a group of Northern Eskimos that were relocated to the area by the government in the 1960s. Flu grew ramped and killed many of them. They were buried on the bluffs of Herendeen Bay, which overlooks the Bearing Sea. High tides have washed away the land exposing graves and it was not uncommon for bones to wash up on the shores. Don had found the skull on the beach and brought it into the lodge. It is small in size and has no dental work done which seems to confirm the story.

After the visitors flew out I went for a walk. It was a very clear and cold day. The ice is on the lake again. I had not noticed from the lodge because this time the ice is frozen clear. I could see the water and bottom of the lake under the ice which gives a strange sensation. I enjoyed the constant moaning sounds the ice made. It was as though the ice was alive.

2/9-10

It snowed off and on all day without much accumulation due to the wind. It is difficult for it to add up when it is snowing sideways.

Now we are having trouble with the marine radio. Pat has been calling but cannot hear our response. It is frustrating to hear him call several times a day, "Bear Lake, Port Moller do you read me?" It bothers me to not have our lifeline but I am sure, in time, someone will grow concerned when we cannot be reached and will fly in to check on us.

I am still having bad dreams. They usually leave me disturbed throughout the day. I think I should put them to good use and start writing horror stories.

17

Wolves

2/19/95

It was cloudy out most of the day but an interesting one. My morning started out routine firing up the generator, enjoying coffee, and writing letters. As I was trying to concentrate on my writing, the dogs were outside barking continuously. They usually bark like this at an eagle, magpie, or fox so I tried to ignore it for a while. But the barking continued and I started feeling like something might be wrong so eventually I decided to go out and see what was going on. I walked around the corner of the lodge towards the direction of the river, where the commotion was coming from and was ecstatic to discover that there was a wolf standing across the river looking back at me. My first thought was wondering whose dog is it when it hit me like a bomb! Wolf! The dogs continued to bark, and I felt that the alpha male across the river stood in an attempt to antagonize the dogs to cross over. I was frozen in my tracks as the wolf stared back at me. Time seemed to stand still and I will never forget the piercing and hypnotizing glare he gave me with his yellow eyes. I was so glad that both dogs did not cross the river to check out the wolf.

When the trance was broken I ran inside to get Rick so he could see him too. Rick was still in bed and when I told him what was going on he jumped up, grabbed the rifle, and ran to the deck. I got mad. Had I known this would be his reaction I would not have shared my discovery with him.

It was then that I noticed there are two other wolves standing in the distance behind the large wolf. The alpha male stood firm and was staring at Rick. I looked over at Rick, he was naked and barefoot standing in the snow while sighting in on his target, the wolf. I wondered how his feet could withstand the snow; adrenalin does amazing things. I shuttered at how this long awaited event was unfolding. Rick fired, and missed. The loud crack of the rifle sent all three of the wolves running. He shot again two more times but missed with all rounds. The wolves were gone from sight and I was thrilled that none appeared to have been shot.

The wolves were beautifully marked with white and gray and to see them in their element was magnificent! I spent the rest of the day looking for them in the spotting scope but never saw them again. I felt bad for how they had been treated yet glad that perhaps this would mean they would stay away from the lodge, people, and the dogs. If I do ever spot them again I will keep it to myself.

18

Nelson Lagoon

2/20/95

Last night after the generator was turned off the discovery of frozen water pipes created another unexpected job for us but after little effort the water was flowing again. I attempted to use the radio and this time it worked long enough for me to discuss the problem with Pat so at least it is known that we are having technical problems and that we are fine. We discussed flying in a different radio. Losing communication here can be life threatening not to mention boring.

It is snowing again and pretty cold out. This has been an unusually cold winter for the peninsula, according to the neighboring residents. I have spent the last few days in the lounge on wolf watch but have not seen any sight of them, or tracks.

2/21

Dailey radioed and stated that she thought I could use a break and Paul offered to fly up and get me so I could spend a few days in Nelson Lagoon.

I liked the idea so I packed and waited for the next fly day. I am excited to meet the people face to face that I have been visiting with for the last six months over the radio. The thought of having luxuries such as a telephone and full time electricity also thrills me along with the flight over and a chance to see some new country.

The next few days passed, the weather has been crummy, and I am starting to get uneasy about leaving the lodge. I am wondering if my apprehension stems from being away from people and civilization for so long. In thinking about it, I had to laugh, like Nelson Lagoon is so civilized with a population in the winter of fifty people.

2/22

I woke to a calm, clear day so I prepared for Paul to fly in, which he did. The flight was awesome as I kept my face pressed against the windows of the super cub looking at all the new sights. I spotted three fox and lots of tracks. The fox really get around across the tundra. We also saw otter or beaver tracks across the top of a frozen pond.

Paul landed the plane in Port Moller and picked up the mail. It was a quick stop and we were on our way again.

Herendeen Bay is beautiful. The mountains and coves are rugged and uninhibited. There is a very old natural hot springs there that I would love to see some time.

We left the mountains behind the closer we came to Nelson Lagoon and out into the open. As we flew across the Bearing Sea I was surprised to see how much ice is in the bays. The patterns of ice consisted mostly of circles and the colors varied from blue, green, gray, and white. The water looks so cold giving an appearance that nothing was alive.

Nelson Lagoon

As we came up on the village I was surprised to see how many houses are standing there. Most of them are quite large and built close together. There are boats sitting in many of the yards and also I was surprised to see so many vehicles.

Nelson Lagoon has been developed on a spit along the Bearing Sea with David River bordering the other side. Paul did not say anything about his intentions, and I did not care, as I was fascinated by everything I was seeing. Paul circled a frozen pond where some young boys were playing ice hockey. To my surprise, Paul touched down which sent the boys laughing and scattering. Without stopping he taxied the length of the pond and lifted back up into the air. Plane games. Paul then stated he was heading to the Fox Den, which is a cabin about seven miles south of the village. He flew low as we slid through the air until we came across a teenage girl who was riding a 4-wheeler headed in the same direction that we were.

She was really cruising across the frozen tundra and it was a task to catch up to her. The super cubs are not known for speed but never the less, I was very impressed with the way she rode her ATV.

We flew low enough that we buzzed over the top of her pulling up at the last minute giving us all a thrill. She laughed and waved as we flew past her. Funny games they play here. We approached the den and I saw quite a few people there while the smoke from a barbecue rose into the frigid air.

As the sound of the plane grew near more people came out from the den waving us in as we circled.

Paul did land and as the plane came to a stop and the engine shut down everyone came to greet us and I will always treasure the warm smiles and friendly greetings as they welcomed me into their world. It was fun to meet them, hear their comments about how I did not look like what I sound like over the radio. They were super fun people and it appeared to be as nice for them as it was for me to have someone new to tease, poke fun at, and talk to.

They insisted that we eat, which we did, while I was fascinated in learning about them and the den. It is a cabin build out on the tundra for an emergency shelter in the case that anyone gets caught away from the village and has trouble or just needs to warm up. It contains oil burning stove, radio, rifle, and it is stocked with canned food, fuel, and water. There are two bunks, several sleeping bags and pillows, a small table and counter, which take up most of the room. They also use it for a getaway so it has become a social center.

After a nice meal and lots of laughs we loaded back up into the plane and lifted up into the air. At the village we circled the well built airstrip, built with gravel and quite large. It is laid out following the shoreline of the Bearing Sea, providing a fantastic view as we descended and came to our final landing.

I helped Paul secure and unload the plane then Paul drove to his and Dailey's home.

2/23

I slept fairly well considering I am sleeping in the top bunk with the kids in their bedroom. It appeared it was different for them too, as when I woke up their five-year old girl, Candice, was peeking her head up over the side rails to get a glimpse of me. She would quickly duck back down when she saw me looking at her, only to be right back in a few short minutes.

I eventually invited her to come up, which she did, but was too shy to talk much. She just kept looking at me with her big brown eyes expressing her curiosity of this strange woman in her bed. I enjoyed a good breakfast as Dailey and I chatted nonstop for the morning. It was though we had known each other always. She is very nice and I am glad to have her for a friend. Dailey offered the phone so I attempted to get in touch with family and friends only to find out most of them were not home. That was a bit of a disappointment but I was going be here for several days and I knew that I would catch them eventually.

Dailey's sister, Sharon, came over to visit and it really impresses me how close the people are here. They are also very friendly and loving. We laughed almost constantly enjoying each other's company.

This afternoon I walked down the sand street to the post office to mail out letters and I chuckled about how much something as simple as going to the post office could mean. When everyday things, like going to the store for example, are taken away you really learn simple appreciation.

I could hardly stand being at the beach and not getting out for a walk so as soon as I had a chance I headed for the shores. Dailey warned me to take a stick with me, as the fox that I might encounter can be aggressive. That surprised me but I took her warning serious as I headed for the beach.

I was totally amazed and thrilled at the treasures that laid there waiting for me. I found ten Japanese glass floats and excited is not even close to describing the word I feel! I am elated to find the glass floats.

I was surprised to see some of the other items laying on the sand such as; hard hats, dishes, clothing, emergency water packets, Japanese and Russian bottles that have all washed ashore from boats gone down. When I touched and examined each item a solemn feeling of sorrow and respect overwhelmed me.

I was also very impressed with the huge seawall of ice that lay between the shore and the sea. I have never seen such huge chunks of ice, which had built a natural wall for as far as I could see.

Bearing Sea Ice

It started to get dark so I headed back thinking that if I lived here I would be out on the beaches every day. It felt so good to be able to walk as far as I wanted to go. With the containment from the rugged terrain at the lodge I was enjoying this new found freedom and I have always loved walking on the beach.

I made plans for the next morning to be back out on the beach as soon as it was light.

The evening ended with a great salmon dinner and several games of scrabble with Dailey, Little Allen, and Leona. I came in last, as usual, but we had great fun as we shared many laughs and a wonderful time.

2/24

I was so excited about getting out on the beach this morning that I kept waking up and had to force myself to try and go back to sleep. It was much too early and dark to get up. It would not be light for hours and besides that I did not want to disturb the sleeping household.

When I could not stand it any longer, I quietly got up, made a cup of coffee, and anxiously waited for it to get light so I could venture out. When that time finally came, no one else was awake in the house or the village for that matter, so I left a note for Dailey and headed out.

I walked through a beach access road and as I came onto the beach I bent down and grabbed a hand full of sand. It is black volcanic sand and is very course and heavy to the touch. I walked down beach in the opposite direction that I had walked the afternoon before and found a place to get on the seaside of the ice wall then continued farther down the beach.

I loved the sounds and sights of the rough huge waves that crashed onto the sand. It was amazing how far I had gone down the beach and I was the only person out there.

After gathering many treasures, consisting mostly of floats and foreign bottles, I headed off the beach back into the village and was more than ready for breakfast.

The afternoon was spent with Dailey as we did a walking tour of the village while she showed me around. I met more people and received several invitations for meals and visits.

One thing that caught my attention was that in every home there was a radio that is constantly turned on. In fact, it appears to be a favorite pass time and game to try and hear each other's conversations. In realizing this it means everyone was also hearing my conversations, over the radio.

Tactics are tried to set secret channels for people to talk private but part if the game is finding the secret preset channel. There really are not any secrets out here.

Now I understood why many of the people have gotten to know me so well without ever have meeting me face to face. In talking with many of them it was like we had known each other for years.

Dailey filled me with history of the village and I was fascinated with everything she shared. There are graves placed around in people's yards, which usually have little fences and or wooden crosses, and trinkets carefully placed on and around them.

Dogs were running loose everywhere. The school is new and a very impressive facility. The classrooms are large and the kids were curious about me as I was led from room to room and introduced.

No one seemed to mind that the classrooms were being interrupted to introduce me to the children. The children are familiar with Bear Lake Lodge and it was fun for us all.

The gymnasium was fabulous and the people of the village use it for recreation.

That evening we drove out to the Fox Den and not only is it strange to be in a vehicle, it felt odd to have somewhere to go. It had been six months since I had been in anything other than an airplane.

There were several other people already at the den and we had a great time with the music blasting as we sang, danced, and laughed the entire time. We went to bed at 4 am this morning. It had been quite some time since I had so much excitement!

2/25

Today was rainy and windy so instead of walking, Dailey drove me around the village and out to the airstrip to wait for the mail plane to come in. A practice for the villagers to do as they depend on supplies that are flown as well as it gives them something to look forward to each day.

After the plane had been unloaded we drove around as I was showed more sights. Dailey pointed out an island on the riverside of the lagoon where sea gulls nest and told me that for centuries the native women have gone there to gather eggs. Dailey described them as the size of large chicken eggs, brown in color with dark spots, and said that she personally does not care too much for them, as they are fairly fishy tasting. That did not sound very appealing to me either.

She then went on to say, that she does like the Arctic Tern eggs as they have a much better flavor and described them as small, blue in color, and also have spots. Dailey stated that they never gather from a nest with more than two or three eggs in it as by then the eggs are too old. I was captivated by the information and history of it all, though decided that I would stick to chicken eggs.

We returned to her house and I was invited by Little Allen to use a four-wheeler and go out on the beach with him to gather glass floats. He had been out riding earlier and found a location that currently had a lot of glass floats lying on the sand.

The changing of the tides could wash them away so of course I was ready and willing to go.

We bundled up and the two of us headed out. The ATV that I was riding did not have brakes making the ride more exciting. I followed Little Allen down the coastline as we crossed several areas that were so rough we really had to work to get through them. I enjoyed the challenge of going up the bank and then back down planning each move carefully knowing that I would not be able to slow down or stop easily.

Little Allen had strapped a plastic clothes basket to the back of his ATV to carry floats in and on the front of his machine a rifle was strapped in place. We rode about 10 miles down the coast until we came onto an area that was so heavy with glass floats that I could not believe my eyes! I felt like a kid picking up Easter eggs while I ran from float to float. They are beautiful glass balls of different colors, shapes and sizes.

We filled the clothes basket with glass floats within minutes then Little Allen picked up a large rubber float that was lying on the beach and strapped it to the back of my machine, cut an opening in it and we quickly filled it as well.

Some of the floats still have the woven netting on them while others are clear. Many have a sand blasted look to them and some had barnacles on them. There are hand blown glass floats while the newer ones have the markings of a mold. Each and every float I picked up was a pure delight and I could not have been more excited!

Little Allen

On our return trip back to the village we stopped at the den to warm our hands and faces, which a cup of coffee did nicely. It was a pleasant break and I understood the critical purpose of the shelter. It was obvious that if a person had been stranded away from the village the den might make the difference of surviving or not. A calendar hangs on the wall inside the cabin and it is den law that every time you enter the den you write your name on the date. This way, the villagers are able to track each other in the case someone does not return.

As we headed back for the last leg of the journey the wind was blowing hard against us and I was getting cold. It was also getting dark. We had a good time and Little Allen got a kick out of me when I picked up a hard hat that was lying on the beach, and wore it for a while. He understood my teasing in wearing it as just prior to me putting it on, he had led me up on the bank and back down a very steep area that caused me to scream when I had no way of slowing down or stopping. We both got a big laugh out of it after I survived.

This evening we went to bed early as we had been staying up until wee hours each night. I teased them as I said good night stating that I would have to go back to the lodge to get some sleep.

19

Back at the Lodge

2/26/95

Several days have passed and now I am starting to get anxious to be back to the lodge. We are waiting for the weather to clear so the flight can be made safely. The morning that Paul decided to go the wind was blowing around 30 knots and he kept changing his mind about going or not. That made me a bit uneasy and thinking back I should have suggested that we wait until he was sure, but I remained silent and let him make the call. He radioed both Port Moller and Bear Lake to see how the weather was in each location and was assured that it was calm, which was the final determining factor in his decision. We fueled the plane, loaded the treasures, said goodbyes, and once again I was up in the air.

This time Paul flew at a much higher elevation and as we crossed the Bearing Sea. I was surprised to see how the ice had changed in the short time that has passed. We crossed Herendeen Bay and as we flew towards Moller Bay the wind picked up severely tossing the small plane around and for the first time in a plane, my stomach was up in my throat.

As we continued I kept looking down viewing the water as cold death. It was intimidating but the real scare was when Paul began throwing a tantrum because of the wind. Over the sound of the engine I could hear him cussing as he began to throw items such as his gloves and hand held radio around in the cockpit. Up until that moment I was not really too frightened but it became apparent that his panic attitude could indeed cause a pilot error resulting in a possible crash and for a brief moment I considered thumping him over the head and attempt flying the plane myself. As I looked down, the feelings of going down in the icy waters of the Bearing Sea made me shudder. I did not want my life to end that way. I thought of my children and how they would feel to learn such horrible news. I stayed quiet and watched him closely from that point on and have never known such relief as I did to see Port Moller airstrip in the distance. I felt at that point, that we would be all right.

We landed at Port Moller with no problem and as we un-boarded the plane my legs were like rubber bands under me as I was still shaking. I made the comment to Paul that he had done a good job, and he said, "There was nothing to it." He did not know how close he came to waking up with a huge headache. We secured the plane and instead of having Pat meet us at the strip and jumped into an older pick up that was parked at the fuel shed. It belongs to Bear Lake Lodge. We only drove a few yards when we heard a loud grinding noise, big clank, and the truck came to a halt. We both got out and looked under the truck to discover that the u-joints had rusted away and the driveline was lying on the ground. It was not Paul's day and the frustration was showing. He radioed Pat and while we waited for him to come to our rescue I walked out on the beach. I was surprised to discover the amount of bear and fox tracks in the sand. Pat arrived and drove us to the cannery to get mail, supplies, and a short visit. I thought it was a good idea hoping that it would give Paul some time to settle down before we finished flying the last leg into the lodge. While we were at Pat's living quarters I noticed a fox dart between buildings so I tapped on the window and to my surprise he came right over to the window. It was then, that Pat admitted that he had been feeding it, which had caused it to be friendly but also somewhat dependent. He asked me if I wanted to try and feed him and of course I did, so Pat gave me a piece of pepperoni stick to offer the red fox. I opened the window and the fox came running as though someone had rung a dinner bell. He looked at me with caution but the tidbit that I was offering was more tempting for him than was the idea of danger. He very gently took the meat from my hand. I could not help but be taken in by the gentle look in his soft brown eyes. After I fed him a few more pieces he went to a spot not far from the window where the sun was shining on the ground and curled up to take a nap. We visited for a short while but the time came that we had to go. Pat tried all the stall tactics he could think of and I recognized how he felt. Being alone has got to be rough but in our case we were fighting the wind and daylight so back to the airstrip we went. This time I was not so anxious to board and even though I knew better, the idea of walking crossed my mind.

Once in the air I was relieved that the wind had settled and the flight to the lodge was simple. We followed the beach up to Bear River then followed the river to the lodge. I was surprised to see all of the ice chunks that had broken in the lake had now jammed up in the river. The ice mass ran almost the entire length of Bear River. I had been hoping to take the skiff down river again, but seeing this clearly showed me that it was out of the question. Cowboy met the plane as though he knew that I would be on board and both he and I were glad for me to be home.

2/27

Even though I will never forget Nelson Lagoon and the people I am happy to be back in my element. I have been cleaning and admiring the glass floats. I am surprised to count over 200 of them and I love each and every one. Many have markings of different a variety so I will try to get information about them when I get back to the mainland. It was though I could feel the history within the glass floats and loved the individuality of each ball as I held it and looked it over.

A few of them had water in them but no apparent crack. I later found out that happens when there is a pin hole in the float and as the net gets heavy with fish it is pulled down into the water. The deeper it goes the more pressure is put on the hollow float. Once the water is inside, it remains. As I felt the tranquility surrounding me I thought about how much I loved this place and life. It is moments like this that I get very apprehensive about going back to town and people.

2/28

Today is the last day of February and I cannot believe how fast the time is going. Only twenty-five days until my planned departure from the lodge. I spend a little time each day preparing to leave. Cowboy rolled in dead fish and even though I bathed him he still stinks. I wish he would stop doing that. He does not like baths and from the look in his eyes knows he will be getting one when he comes in smelling like that. Other than spotting a single moose on Falcon Crest, it has been pretty still around here.

3/1

A lump rose in my throat the day the radio call came in that Laurie had made all arrangements for me to leave the lodge and fly to Oregon. She will send my tickets in the mail. It is going to be hard to leave the lodge and go back to civilization. As the days grow closer, I am actually becoming scared of the idea. I have grown so comfortable in my world and the thought of store bought and fast food is grossing me out. Also thinking about riding in a car and dealing with traffic is bothering me. Rick and Cowboy will be staying behind for a few weeks longer, and then we will meet back up in Kenai. I am not real concerned about Rick, but Cowboy will not understand and because he sticks to me like glue it upsets him when I leave without him. He pouts and makes me feel bad.

3/2

We have been having some beautiful days and the temperature rose today to sixty-one degrees! It feels like spring.

3/5

I was out enjoying the spring weather when I heard the familiar buzz of a plane and as the Cub circled I could see Allen and Arlene on board. What a pleasant surprise. Arlene and I had a nice visit while Allen flew Rick over to Port Moller to get mail and a break from the lodge. It is always such a wonderful treat to have a visitor.

Allen told me that he thought there was an old satellite receiver around here so I searched the basement and did find a rather antique looking thing. It took two days of tinkering to figure it out and when we did we were only able to receive a few stations, but anything was better than nothing. I really did not mind the quiet but the link to the outside world is an advantage, I guess. Of the few stations that we do receive, court TV and the OJ trial is one of the options of all things. As I watch the proceedings I believe that he is guilty and have a horrible feeling that he is going to get away with it. It is terrible. My heart aches for the family and friends of the victims.

3/6

The days continue to stay nice and for the most part, calm. We took the skiff out on the lake but did not get far due to ice. There is a very clear thin layer and we tried to forge through it but the sound of it hitting the aluminum sides of the skiff is like a finger nail on a chalk board so we turned back. A good decision I am sure. I had hoped to get to the head to the lake one more time before leaving the lodge but it is appearing like that might not happen.

I spend a great deal of time out on the deck, basking in the sun, listening to the ice crack, watching and listening for animals, but all I have seen lately are fox.

One nice thing about having the TV back on is I have been tracking the Iditarod Dog Race. It was fun to see the start of the race. The dogs are excited and cannot wait to start running. They are making record time this year.

Cowboy watching the start of the Iditarod Dog Race

3/8

I am thrilled at the amount of daylight we are gaining. I laugh that my life has become so simple and uneventful that the big excitement of the day is to time sunrise and sunset.

I decided to go for a walk downstream so put on the chest waders and the dogs and I headed out on another adventure. At the point that I decided to cross the river I got about hip deep only to find my pants wet and boots filled with water. The glue in the seam of the waders had come apart so the waders served no purpose. My first thought was that I would have to turn back but decided to continue as the day was warm and I did not want a little water to spoil my trip. Because the temperatures have been so warm I have started packing the rifle on my ventures again.

The extra weight of wet clothes and full boots gave me a good work out and I thought about making it a habit. I followed lots of fox tracks and came onto a small pack of wolf tracks. They are probably the same wolves that had come to the lodge. There is no mistaking the tracks from dog or fox, as they are so large.

Each bend that I rounded held anticipation that I might spot them but as expected, did not. At one point the dogs had gotten quite a distance ahead of me and began barking like crazy. When I finally caught up to them the mighty two, had cornered and were harassing a porcupine. Unwisely I said to Cowboy, "what is it?' And of course he had to show me, henceforth four quills in his face. I felt responsible and was glad to see that they were not in very far; I was able to pull them out with my fingers right there. He was really mad at the quilled varmint and even though I walked on, the dogs would not call off and follow me.

I went back to the lodge and Cowboy showed up later with yet another quill. I could not believe that he would be so stubborn. In most cases dumb would be the word but in his, I know that he has the attitude that he can do better if he tries harder. I have seen it over and over with him. This time the quill was in his lower lip and I know it was painful to remove. It was painful for me anyway.

3/9

We are still having sunny days. Even though the wind is blowing between fifteen and twenty mph we got a radio call from Allen stating that he was going to fly to Port Moller, get our mail, and pick up Pat so that he could get away on an outing. It was a very enjoyable visit for us all but especially Pat, as he had not left the cannery all winter and has never been to the lodge. Pat brought some movies with him for us to borrow. We will enjoy them as we have already watched all of the movies that are here and some twice.

As always, Allen is such a joy to be around. He has such an easy going personality, yet he is funny and we enjoy his presence immensely.

I have been making moose and caribou jerky in the oven. Rick does not like it stating it tastes like liver, but it does not. I distaste liver and could not eat it if it even came close to it. Allen and Pat liked it so I sent some with them. The ovens needed cleaning after making jerky and it took hours.

3/10

It has cooled off again and the ice is staying on the lake. It does not look like any more skiff trips are in the cards.

The heater stopped working this evening so we took the regulator apart and it was full of water. After that was cleaned out, it lit again. There is never a dull moment around here. I also have not been having very good luck getting the main generator started the last few mornings so I have been running the portable generator until Rick gets up. I prefer not to use the noisy generator sitting on the porch and I am getting tired of things not working around here. If all else was not enough the toilet overflowed today. What a mess, the area is carpet. No plumber to call so one has to learn the hard way and become creative as parts are not always available. If you cannot find it here you have to make something work, or do without.

3/13

I was lying on the bed reading and looked out the window just in time to see a fox run past. It was nice to see, as I had not seen any living thing in quite awhile. He is the typical red and white color but I noticed that his coat seemed very dull. I am wondering if he is sick and hoped the dogs would not get a hold of him.

Last night I dreamt that I had been shot several times and my attackers were standing over me, watching and waiting for me to die. When I did not die, they began shooting again. It was horrible and I feel I now know what animals go through when they are hunted.

The Iditarod update showed the lead musher; Doug Sweenly was expected to arrive in Nome tomorrow. He is from Montana and my nephew, Jason, trains under him. That is exciting.

3/14

It has been real cold out. Last nights' coldest temperature was minus eight and only warmed up to minus six during the day. The big news around the state was the cold temperatures that were breaking records in several areas. There was a one hundred and four degree difference between the temperature in the panhandle registering at fifty-four degrees and the north-slope measuring fifty below. The sun does not necessarily mean warmth.

I have been working on a leather trapper style cap for Rick for his birthday. It is easy to find time to work on it without him around. The cap is coming along well even though I do not have any large fur scraps to work with so I am patching beaver pieces together to make the front and ear sections.

The excitement of the day was a pretty big earthquake that shook the lodge around 8:30 this morning. It was a rolling one and it felt like it went on for a long time. I got caught trying to remember what the rules of safety for quakes are. I could not really remember so I just stood there enjoying it.

I went outside after it stopped to check the fuel lines making sure that they were all still connected which they were, then went up into the lounge and was surprised to discover that all of the items hanging in the rafters were still swinging. After spending the winter here I have gained a big respect for the forces of nature. Natural power has never seemed so obvious anywhere I have been before now.

3/15

Today along with the remaining cold temperatures the wind blew causing the chill factor to lower to minus forty-four. It is bitterly cold and the wind stings my face and hands when I go outside. As I walked to the generator shed this morning the cold wind sucked my breath away making me feel like I was holding my breath. I had to hurry to get inside the shed so I could breathe. A person would not last long out here today. I wonder how the animals are able to survive these extremes.

We decided to leave the generator running in hopes of avoiding frozen lines while it remains cold like this. Our latest concern is that we are getting low on diesel fuel.

3/17

It has been a real treat getting up to electricity with the generator running. Such luxury. Our efforts only partially paid off as the water line and drain in the kitchen have now frozen. I spent all day working on the frozen pipes and have cold water running now, but no hot and the drain is still frozen. It could be worse; at least I am enjoying the snow that is now falling.

A very scary incident happened in Nelson Lagoon today and as the panic call came over the radio I shivered. John Jr. was riding his snow machine on the river and fell through the ice. No one could see him in the fog and the screaming and crying was very hard to listen to. The situation ended with a relief as he did make it out of the water and was on the opposite side of the river. His sled however stayed in the water, but even though he was wet and very cold, he was rescued alive.

3/18

I am tired of the frozen pipes so I decided to attempt plumbing and my first attempt was to boil water and pour it down the drain and plunge. It appeared to be working only to look down and see the water pouring out all over the floor. Now on top of the frozen pipes, I have a big mess to clean up. Rick's attitude is they will thaw when it warms up. That was not acceptable to me so I took the plastic pipes apart which was a mistake as I still did not get the water flowing and now I cannot get the pipes back together.

I push on one side and it falls out on the other. All the joints leak and I have made matters worse. After spending hours on the project I went to Rick and asked him to please come and help me. He said that I took them apart, so I can put them back together. It took the rest of the day, but I finally did get things back together with minimal leakage. The pipes are still frozen and the dishes are piling up. I will take it apart again tomorrow. What a mess.

3/19

I spent all of this morning finishing the trapper's cap. I am glad to have it done.

Gunner radioed and we had a nice visit. We talked about the kitchen pipe situation and he suggested that I use electrical tape to put the pipes back together and that is what I did.

This time the pipes went back together better and no leaks. I guess I am gaining experience, wanted or not. The temperature outside has warmed up to twenty degrees and the hot water thawed on its own so I went to work on the drain. I filled the sink with hot water and began plunging. It eventually worked and it was quite a thrill to see the water whirlpool as it flowed down the drain. I feel good about the accomplishment and the fact that the dishes are now done once again. Another lesson in taking every day life for granted.

3/20

I woke this morning at 5:30 to find Rick still up for the night. It is just a few more days until my departure now and I am more nervous than ever.

3/21

Paul radioed today stating that he was flying to Port Moller and asked if I was ready to fly out. I thanked him but told him no. Allen and I had already made arraignments for my departure and I had made up my mind that I did not want to fly with Paul again unless there was no other choice.

Paul did bring in our mail but did not show up until 7 pm, which meant he only stayed long enough to unload the plane and take off.

The mail delivery brought in a card from Lars and Marit stating that they were at Port Heiden and doing well. It was great to hear from them and as I followed their tracks on the map I was impressed with the distance they had traveled since leaving the lodge.

3/22

Today was calm but very gray out. The clouds are hanging low giving everything the appearance of black and white. I sat in the lounge most of the day and was thrilled to see a river otter that had come up river to fish. He stayed most of the afternoon out in front of the lodge and it was very entertaining to watch him dive down and come up somewhere else in the broken ice. The otter seemed very playful, as his actions did not appear to be all work.

We put a few pieces of frozen salmon along the shore to attempt to lure him closer, which worked even though he did not take the bait. The magpies did have a good meal out of it and it was funny to watch them slip and slide as they flew in and around the fish.

The otter continued to entertain me most of the day finally coming close enough several times to get a really good look at him. He was large and was quite mischievous. The lake is still very frozen but the river is open now.

Allen radioed and we confirmed plans for the following day, weather permitting; he would be up to get me. It felt really weird, extremely bittersweet.

3/23

I did not get much sleep last night. I have real mixed emotions about leaving. The weather looked like it was going to cooperate with the plans and I was not sure I wanted it too. I prepared to leave only to get a radio call from Allen saying he could not get off the ground at Nelson Lagoon due to high winds. Cold Bay was also having severe winds that grounded Penn Air, which was rare. The news of bad weather was strange because the weather is so calm here.

I was sitting and looking out the window when I saw the sickly fox walk past the lodge again. This time it was obvious that the fox had a problem so I told Rick about it and he went out and shot it. I agreed this time, that it was for the best.

While Rick was skinning her the hide on her tail crumbled and fell off. The hide was completely dried and dead. That was freaky.

20

Leaving the Bush

3/24/95

Today is the day I have been waiting for. Allen radioed about noon inquiring about the weather at the lodge and stated that he would be over to get me. As soon as I heard the buzz of the plane, my eyes began to tear up.

Allen preparing for my departure

It was very hard for me to leave and it tore at my heart when we taxied lifting up in to the sky. I watched as I lost sight of my dog, the lodge, and my life.

The flight its self was nice. Allen is a great pilot it is a treat to fly with him. It is like he and the plane become one. We spotted two moose and some otter tracks. Herendeen Bay was frozen but most of the Bearing Sea is opened. There are still large chunks of ice floating in it. As we approached Nelson Lagoon I was surprised to see that all along the coast line was frozen. I am still amazed that salt water can freeze. Arlene was waiting for us at the airstrip as the wind began to blow. Arlene had prepared a tasty roast beef dinner for us and after gorging our selves Leona and I walked over to Paul and Dailey's storage shack where Dailey had told me earlier that she would be there, hanging.

I expected that to be the term they use for hanging out but as we entered the building I realized that it is the term used for working on their fishnets. Dailey had the stereo blasting while she sat on a special hand-made stool and I was fascinated while I watched her work. Dailey's movements were so swift and graceful as she weaved back and forth tying the led line to the net. The weight of the led line is what keeps the bottom of the net down. I asked Dailey to show me how to weave the net and she was happy to teach me. We all laughed at how slow and awkward I was at weaving it yet it was awesome to learn. Daily said I just needed practice and to come back anytime so I could get some. I think I was being had. We hung for a while then we talked her into coming with us to the den for one last night of fun before I left. Dailey was glad to go and about a group of twelve showed up as we spent the evening dancing, laughing, and singing until wee hours of the morning.

Then misfortune struck. In a wild moment of jumping up in the air, Dailey came down on her foot and it rolled over as we all heard the dreaded snap. It was an awful sound that her ankle made. Dailey said that it was sore but not too bad and refused to call an end to the night not wanting to spoil the fun. Around 4 am we decided to call it good.

3/25

Now that I have left the lodge I am getting excited about flying out and seeing my family and friends. I only slept a few hours and as usual was the first person to get up so I made coffee and as the house came to life my excitement grew.

When I thought Dailey would be awake I walked over to her house to check on her and her injury. It was obvious that it hurt terribly as it was swollen and bruised. She would need to fly to Anchorage today to have it taken care of. I felt so bad for her.

We took her to the airstrip to meet the Mark Air commuter flight into Anchorage. Just getting her into the plane was a rough job. Dailey was in a great deal of pain by now and every movement was hard for her. As they taxied, she waived and it was sad to have our good byes end on that note.

Penn Air was scheduled to pick me up so we called the office in Cold Bay to find out when they would be arriving in Nelson Lagoon to get me. The agent informed us that the plane would be arriving between 4 and 5 pm. When the plane did not show up on time I began to get nervous. I had another flight to catch out of Cold Bay that evening and we were pushing it.

We got tired of waiting at the airstrip so went back to the house, called Cold Bay again and they assured us that the plane would be here and would have me in Cold Bay in time to catch my connecting flight. We visited for a little while longer than drove back out to the airstrip to meet the plane. I was very surprised at the amount of people that came out to the strip to see me off. It was very meaningful.

The plane came into sight and finally it was time for me to get on board. I was the only passenger so I got to ride co-pilot, or second seat, as it is called in the industry.

The plane is a Cherokee and it flew much faster and differently than the super cubs that I had grown accustomed to. Once we were in the air the pilot told me he had mail on board for Port Moller so we headed there first before going to Cold Bay. By this time I was down-right worried about catching my flight. I voiced my concerns and the pilot assured me that we would have plenty of time. It only took about ten minutes to fly to Port Moller compared to about thirty in the Piper Cub. As Port Moller came into view I could look over to see the mountains of Bear Lake and it haunted me. I considered having the pilot fly me back to the lodge but fought the urge thinking of my waiting family.

We made a quick stop, it was nice to say good-bye to Pat in person and in a flash we were back up in the air. Most of the flight was covered in fog so we rose above the clouds to a higher elevation in which the sky was clear. I enjoyed being able to observe the control panel as well as taking in any of the sights possible. It was sunny and warm above the clouds making me sleepy.

The Alaskan Peninsula is so narrow in places that there were times that I could see the Bearing Sea on one side and the Pacific Ocean on the other. Occasionally steep and rugged mountain peaks would pop their heads out above the clouds. I could see Cold Bay in the distance while we crossed a canyon, which created heavy turbulence. The plane was dropping and bobbing from side to side. I looked at the pilot and he was not showing any signs of having "Paul syndrome", so I assumed everything was fine, which it was. With the Cold Bay runway in sight, I was getting excited about finishing the second leg of my journey and heading toward the third.

It was interesting to land on the 10,400-foot runway that Cold Bay hosts. The pilot informed me that the runway is an alternate landing strip for the space shuttle and was built by the military during WWII. It did not take long to see that the impressive runway was about the only thing that Cold Bay offered. The place is very small and looks like a real dive. Rolling on the ground we taxied over to a huge hanger as the large door opened. The plane was parked inside while a friendly Dalmatian dog greeted us. I had not seen any other plane on the tarmac and when I asked the pilot about it all he said was to go into the office and talk to them. I had a feeling that something was going array and at that point, I doubted that I was getting out of Cold Bay tonight.

Inside I was told that the plane was grounded in Dutch Harbor due to high winds. The next plane to Anchorage would not be in until Monday and today is Saturday. I was shocked and at the least unhappy. What that meant was I am stranded here in this dump when I could have at least stayed in Nelson Lagoon where I had a place to stay and people I knew. From there I was sent over to the Mark Air office, which is the airline that I am scheduled to fly out on. The manager was polite and sympathetic about my situation and like me, very un-happy with Penn Air for picking me up; as they knew all along I would not be able to get out of Cold Bay. Discussing the situation and options he considered flying me back to Nelson Lagoon, but said if he did that I probably would not get out until Wednesday. Mark Air is also dealing with a shortage of aviation fuel, which he was hesitating to use for this purpose. He asked if I would accept a room at the local motel at their expense and I would be able to get out on Monday. I did not have much choice so appreciating his help he set me up for two nights in the motel.

I called my daughter to advise her of my situation. She was also disappointed.

Next I called Allen and Arlene and they also were very upset at Penn Air and the situation, and Arlene told me that the lodge has an account at the store and café here in Cold Bay instructing me not to hesitate to use them. That was a relief as money was the one thing I was not over loaded with.

My room is a real dump. It is clean and I am thankful for that but it is only about a 10x10 room with no TV or bathroom. The rate is one hundred dollars a night and I would not be pleased about it if I were paying the atrocious price.

The bathroom facilities are down the hall. I spent the rest of the evening on the pay phone, which was located outside of the bar in the motel. While I spoke with an agent from Mark Air attempting to reschedule my flights, two earthquakes hit. Everyone in the bar started whooping and hollering but it only irritated me as I was in no mood to enjoy the quakes even warped as I am. When the ticket agent heard all the noise she asked what was going on and I said "Oh it is just an earthquake" then seconds later the quake hit Anchorage and the agent. She was not so calm and hung up on me. Eventually with new arrangements in place, I went to my room to sulk.

3/26

At least I woke to a beautiful day here in Cold Bay. Good weather is rare for here as the average nice days a year are ten, hence the name. It is almost always cloudy, windy, and rainy. The temperature stayed around forty so it felt warm out as well. I went to the cafe for coffee and breakfast. The food was not very good and the prices were terrible. Like the motel, the café was the only one in town. Greed is a terrible thing. I visited with others in the cafe and was told there is a library, community recreation center, and a church so after eating I walked down to the recreation center and took my frustrations out on exercise equipment. The facility is new and very nice including a weight room and a racquetball court. And there is no charge for using the equipment. I was the only one there and was glad to have the place to myself.

From there I went over to the church, which is held in an old military Quonset hut. It was nice yet strange to be around people.

While I walked around town I was surprised to see how many fox are running around. They appear to be quite tame as I stood and watched one dig a tunnel in a pile of dirt left by construction. The fox did not seem bothered by my presence at all. He stretched lazily and yawned as I walked within about twenty feet of him.

I watched as a Coast Guard helicopter brought in someone that had been injured on a crab boat. He was transferred onto a Coast Guard jet and flown to Anchorage.

After that I walked to the library and checked out a book about the Peninsula. Back in my room I enjoyed reading and learning more history about the places that I have grown accustomed to. The peninsula evolved from erupting volcanoes and the ground is considered young. That is why there are so many earthquakes. Archeological artifacts suggest that humans reached the peninsula around 9,000 years ago and are of Asian descent. There is a natural hot spring in Moller Bay where they have found large piles of clamshells aging thousands of years back. Eventually Russian fur traders and Scandinavian fishermen began showing up and married many of the Aleut women. The book spoke a lot about Nelson Lagoon and it was fun to read about and see pictures of people that I know.

I ate dinner, had a hot shower, read some more, and fell asleep hoping that I will get out of here tomorrow.

3/27

Just as I feared, I woke up often and early and ultimately could not go back to sleep. I was hoping to sleep in to make my time here shorter but not the case. The plane was not due to depart until 3 pm so waking up at 5:30 am did not please me too much.

Around 8 am I went to the cafe for breakfast then made one last call to Allen and Arlene to update them on what was happening. After the store opened I bought some shampoo and toothpaste, showered, and was out of the motel by the 11 am check out time. I took my bags over to the Mark Air Terminal and confirmed my flight plans for the day.

A fish processing plant was shutting down for the season in Sand Point and Mark Air was busy shuttling in cannery workers to catch the same flight out. The small terminal filled up fast and was very over crowded. Most of the people did not speak English. People and luggage were scattered, stacked, and lying in every available inch of the terminal.

I started chatting with a teenage girl from King Cove which helped pass the time. A man from Honduras began talking with us and he was interesting to listen to. He told us about his country and the life there and it sounds terribly violent and scary. I guess I should be thankful to be in Cold Bay and not Honduras.

I walked over to the Post Office to see if there was any mail for me and there was. It all helped pass the time.

Finally the boarding process began. Going through the security check took forever as we stood in line for a very long time. Every seat on the jumbo jet was filled, making the plane crowded and stinky. I thought we would never arrive into Anchorage and when we finally did, I had to run to the gate to make my next flight.

The flight from Anchorage was awful as the seats are so cramped that I could not sit straight due to my knees hitting the seat in front of me. I felt sorry for anyone who was taller than I am, as I was very uncomfortable. Nothing was served to eat or drink, but in the end, I was glad to be on board.

The sights flying out of Anchorage are breathtaking with the majestic mountains and glaciers. They seemed to go on forever showing the vast undeveloped and rugged country. We made a stop in Juneau which was interesting. Because of the mountains, the planes have to come in at an angle which requires a sharp turn just as it lines up with the runway. Quite thrilling actually. It is beautiful with large trees and lots of surrounding islands. I thought it would be a nice place to live if only it did not rain so much.

By the time I reached Seattle I was roasting and peeling off the layers of clothing. The terminal was busy and the hustle and bustle was almost more than I could stand. I felt like I was in a herd of cattle. Everyone was moving fast around me and I felt out of place. I found my way to my final leg of my journey and finally, was on the plane headed to Portland. I shook my head as I thought about taking five different planes to get here.

Cherry and my granddaughter, Hailey, met me at the airport and it was wonderful to see them.

I could smell the stink of the city and the fast movements of the traffic made me dizzy. A few times I had to close my eyes to keep from spinning while we traveled on the freeway. Except for the brief rides in Nelson Lagoon, I had not been in a car for eight months. I guess it will take some getting used to. I thought it strange how I did not notice the smell, noise, or traffic when I lived in Portland. Realizing all of this assured me that I hoped I never had to live in a big city again.

21

Summer Break

The summer was a busy one and went by fast. I enjoyed my visit in Oregon. My second grandson, Trevor, was born while I was there, and I was thankful to be able to be with my son and his wife for the big event. It was hard to leave family and friends but I was ready to get back to Alaska.

My return trip was a hassle as I got caught up in the Mark Air financial mess. They went out of business in the time period I was in Oregon leaving a lot of people stranded, and I was one of them. It took hours on the phone and finally Northwest Air made an agreement to accept my Mark Air ticket if one hundred dollars was added to the fare so at least I did not have to pay full fair to return home to Alaska.

Finally I was back in Kenai. We stayed at Laurie Johnson's house while she was out at the lodge. This home was also built by her father, Don; it is a beautiful home and is located on the bluff overlooking the Cook Inlet straight across from Lake Clark Pass.

The Aleutian Mountain Range across the inlet provides fantastic scenery and views. You can see several live volcanoes in the range and I enjoy just sitting and looking. The sound of the waves at night usually put me to sleep.

We discovered a way to get down to the beach from the house so I go down as often as possible.

Most of the summer has been consumed with working. I took a waitress job in a little cafe that I worked at for about a month before we went to the lodge last fall. It is five miles out of Kenai in a fishing area. They serve good food and the cafe stays busy.

Rick worked for a surveyor then worked "turn around" which is the term used at a chemical plant in North Kenai. The plant shuts down every year to check and replace valves. The job only lasted for a few weeks but the money was very good with a lot of overtime wages.

We are now residents of Alaska and allowed to subsistence fish so we gathered equipment; a set net and stakes and threw them down the bank. It was awesome as we worked with the tide, staking our net and waiting for the fish. We were able to see fish hit the net so fearing we might get more than we could use, we pulled it. Hauling the fish and equipment back up the hill was not nearly as fun but the fish were worth it.

Two very sad and horrible events took place over the summer. First, Peter Faust, the man that came out to Bear Lake Lodge with Gunner, crashed his super cub on Mt. Eklutna. He had been reported missing but his plane was not located for several weeks. It was finally spotted nose down on the north side of the mountain and had burned. The news was very disturbing.

The next tragic event broke my heart. We lost our dear friend Allen. I was horror-struck when the call came in that he had drowned while fishing. His wife, Arlene, had fallen overboard into the bitterly cold water of the river. Allen knowing she could not swim jumped in to save her. He was successful in getting her to a buoy but then he went down, and did not come back up.

Allen Nelson
Rest in peace our dear friend.

22

Return to the Lake

10/21/95

Because of our great love of Bear Lake we have agreed to go back to the lodge for a second winter season. I have spent most of the day making final preparations for the departure. This year we will be flying out in a Cessna 180 owned by a friend of the Johnson's, Skip White. When he can get away from his regular job at Unocal he flies for the lodge. We are scheduled to fly out tomorrow so I have been busy taking advantage of things like a telephone and last minute shopping. I am glad to be done at the café for the season and anxious to get back to the lodge and out of the city. I have missed the peace and solitude of lodge life.

Things will be very different this year without Allen. His presence is certainly missed by many.

10/23

Last night the wind kicked up and blew all night. Skip called this morning stating that the flight would be rough but thought that we could give it a try. We met at the Kenai Airport, loaded our things in his plane then went to a local restaurant to have breakfast while we waited for it to get light.

Skip also was keeping a close eye on the weather report before making the final decision to go or not. One last phone call confirmed that the winds in Homer were blowing forty-five knots at the 3,000-foot elevation, which meant it is not worth the risk. Lake Clark Pass is risky at best and there is no reason to put our lives in jeopardy. We went back to the plane and put together an overnight bag then settled back in, hoping to get out the following morning.

Skip White's Cessna

The last few days have remained windy and freezing rain was falling over Illiminia and Lake Clark Pass, so we stayed on the east side of the peninsula, waiting and watching.

While I sat on the couch looking across the inlet at the world that was tugging at me I could not help feeling inspired by the Aleutian Mountain Range as it is so gorgeous and inviting. I have spent many hours sitting here staring over at it.

From a distance I heard the buzz of airplanes approaching and then it began to sound like we were under attack. In fact we were, one by one, the Bear Lake planes took their turn landing at the hanger across the highway. It was most of the gang from the lodge. I drove over to greet them and provide assistance in unloading and hauling equipment.

They were thrilled to have their season behind them and as they shared their excitement to be back in town I could not help but think that they are crazy. I feel just the opposite and cannot wait to get out of here.

10/25

We were finally able to fly out today and the flight went very well. As we entered Lake Clark Pass the turbulence was heavy which is expected until we round the corner inside the pass. The sun was just coming up on the mountaintops as we flew by showing a lovely shade of pink.

Lake Clark Pass

The mountains and glaciers have a much different look to them this time, as it is almost a month later that we are flying out compared to last year. We have had several snowfalls this year and the ice is forming. Knowing more about what to expect this time, I could feel the world ahead of me.

In the area of King Salmon we flew into some fog but got through it just fine.

The animals have joined up in herds for their winter migrations. We saw thousands of geese and swans and there were many large herds of caribou.

We followed the shores of the Bearing Sea and I was delighted to recognize the sights. Skip turned the plane towards the lodge and the terrain was familiar territory. From a distance, I was thrilled to see the lodge buildings and lake as we approached our winter destination.

The landing strip was very muddy and sloppy from the large amounts of rain that had fallen this past season. Marlie, Warren's wife, met us at the plane and the unloading process began. Without Laurie there, no lunch was waiting so I prepared a quick meal for Skip so that he would not have to fly back to Kenai without eating.

Marlie and her daughter decided that a departing plane was more than they could resist and quickly gathered their last minute items to make the return flight with Skip.

Shortly after we arrived Warren landed in the Super Cub with the last hunter that remained from the season. He would have been going home empty handed from his attempted bear and caribou hunt had Warren not spotted a dead walrus lying on the beach which provided him with a very valuable trophy; ivory tusks. Besides Warren and the hunter, only one guide was still at the lodge and the three of them flew out the following morning. I waved as they lifted up and headed off into the distance to get back to their worlds, leaving us to ours.

10/28

We spent our first full day setting ourselves up and taking inventory of the food and other items, such as the first aid kit and other necessities.

The freezers and pantries are nicely stocked again. As I continued with the clean and set up in the lounge I noticed a King Fisher land on the deck. I spotted some tracks in the sand so went out to take a closer look. They resembled bear but much smaller so I compared them to some mounted animals in the lounge and I think that they are wolverine tracks. I hope to see one of those nasty critters, I think.

Warren told us that a lot of wolves have been spotted in the area this year and asked us to kill any of them that we see as he feels they are interfering with the success of his hunts. I did not respond but you can count on me for not shooting any, as well as, if I spot even signs of them, I will not share my findings with Rick. I hope Cowboy does have any contact with the wolves, only one of the many risks in coming here.

I shuttered at the story Warren had told about having a Labrador dog that he had taken with him on a hunt and left tied to the skiff only to find the dog dead when Warren returned. Wolves had killed the tied and helpless dog. I have read that when a domestic dog joins up with a pack of wolves what usually happens is the dog could be allowed to run with the pack but because the dog does not know the wolf pack rules it will end up disobeying and be killed by the pack.

10/29

The last few days have been busy for us as we continued to get unpacked and settled. We have been receiving a lot of radio calls from people in Nelson Lagoon and Pat at Port Moller welcoming us back. It was comforting, and I felt like I was home.

The wind kicked up and blew hard through the night and all day. The lake is really churning with gusts blowing up into the seventy mph range. A lot of rain is falling also.

The skiff was left on the beach too close to the lake and the rough waters have swamped it. It is completely filled with water. I went out and removed the oars and gas tank before they floated downstream. Rick did not want to open the hanger door as the wind could blow it off the tracks which of course would be an even bigger problem so he set a second anchor on the skiff and we will deal with it after the storm passes.

10/30

Today was much calmer so the skiff was pulled up on the beach with the Kubota tractor and the water was drained. The motor started and no damage was done so we decided to take the skiff out for a cruise thinking it would be good to run the motor and we went around the entire lake. The fall colors are beautiful and the area is abundant with ducks and eagles. We spotted two bears on the west side of the lake. The sow ran off immediately but the cub stayed longer and I was very impressed by his shimmering blonde coat. I had heard about bears with this color of fur but had not seen one until now. The golden color of the bear is gorgeous and sparkling in the sun.

We will probably not see as many bears this season due to the fall hunt that just ended. Bear season in Alaska alternates from spring one year to fall the next year. There was a fall hunt this year so the bears will be much more nervous while things calm down.

As we rounded the head of the lake and came upon the creek that we like to walk up, we spotted a second sow and cub that has a beautiful chocolate colored coat. It was the deepest brown color that I have seen on a bear. What a treat, both rare bear colors in one day. This sow ran off abruptly leaving her cub behind who did not seem bothered by our presence and continued to fish. I love it when they do not run away so that I can watch them without feeling like we are a disturbance.

Making our way back to the lodge, we spotted a large covey of ptarmigan sitting in an alder thicket. They had no intention of flying away as we approached. We were close enough that we could have thrown rocks at them. They are not very smart birds.

10/31

Tonight is Halloween. No tick or treaters this year and I have not seen my little magpie buddy but I think of her often especially during special occasions when she would get treats. I enjoyed carving the pumpkin and roasting the seeds. I made cup cakes and enjoyed a nice radio conversation with Maxi from Nelson Lagoon. He is one of my many favorite people from the village and I am excited to be with everyone again.

There is not much firewood here this year so we spent a few days driving the Kubota tractor around gathering whatever wood we could find lying around. It was not much. I found a nice primary feather from an adult eagle making the day complete.

11/1

Rick got the ranger out of the hanger and we had fun playing on it. He pulled up to the window and was clowning around, showing off like a teenage boy. It is a wild piece of machinery. The ranger is built with six wheels that set on cat tracks, and you steer it with levers that apply brakes. It has two old metal tractor seats, which are mounted one behind the other, and its use is primarily to pack meat. It travels across the tundra and swamps very well, being a critical piece of equipment for the hunting guides. The thing just cracks me up. We are able to cross the backwaters with it and head out across the tundra opening up a new and farther world for us to explore. I do not know why we did not use it last year.

We spotted three moose by Falcon Crest and it is great to see the place so alive.

11/2

The generator would not start this morning and a broken switch was discovered to be the problem. Here we go again I thought. Rick radioed Pat asking him to call the dealership in Anchorage for some information. They gave Pat instructions to bypass the switch, which worked and we are back in business. I was looking through the spotting scope down river, and as I scanned the countryside several miles out, to my astonishment, I spotted a real wild, black, white, and brown animal.... Cowboy! Although I was not thrilled at finding him that far away from the lodge I really was not all that surprised.

11/4

The temperatures have been lowering and the pleasant surprise of snow fell during the night. That is always fun to wake up to.

We have been playing with a remote controlled boat in the lake but today I got out of control and hit a rock bending the rudder. Now it will only go around in circles. It got me in the mood to go for a boat ride so I talked Rick into taking me down river in the skiff while the water is still deep enough to take such an excursion.

There are a lot of dead stinky fish rotting along the shores so I am sure Cowboy will be getting a lot of baths this year.

We came to an eagle's nest, which is built in a single standing alder, and I asked Rick to take me to shore so that I could look for feathers around the nest. The river water was rushing and as we got by the shore Rick asked me if I could jump to the bank, which I tried, unsuccessfully. Into the cold and swift water I went. It was much deeper than I expected. I hit bottom with water up to my chest and I was scared I was going to get cut by the boat propeller while I was being pushed by the current. My body was instantly cold as I pulled myself up on shore. Cowboy brought some bear tracks to my attention so I cautiously walked over to the nest and found three small feathers and two white tail feathers. Well worth the trip, even though it meant I was now wet.

Back in the boat I was really cold but did not admit it so I was relieved when Rick turned the skiff back and we started the trip upstream. On the way back we got into shallow waters twice that required us to get out and drag the skiff against the current then jump back in while it was moving in an attempt not to lose grounds.

I can feel several bruises on my legs from boat hopping. It was very tiring and when we rounded the bend placing the dock in sight I was happy. Coffee, soup, and dry clothes brought me back as good as new except for being tired and sore.

I spent the evening looking through the spotting scope and found a large covey of ptarmigan by Falcon Crest and two bears. The first bear I spotted was fishing on the west side of the lake when the second bear appeared and chased the first bear from the fishing hole.

As I watched the bear run away, I continue to be amazed at the amount of ground that a bear can cover in such a short time. Before retiring for the evening I watched the episode of "I Love Lucy" where she, Ricky, Ethel, and Fred went to Nome, Alaska. The guest star was Red Skelton and I sure enjoyed it.

11/5

Warren told us that he had made arrangements with Penn Air to bring in mail and supplies this year so I spent all day staying close to the radio knowing that today is the day Penn Air will fly to Nelson Lagoon, Port Moller, last stop, Bear Lake Lodge.

Penn Air did not come so I radioed Pat, who then called Penn Air in Cold Bay, only to be told that they did not know anything about such arrangements. We will have to get a hold of Warren and get this miscommunication straightened out.

11/6

The weather has been beautiful out. Sunny yet cool with temperatures in the teens.

Walking today I followed a game trail that led me past a beautiful frozen waterfall then continued following the trail as it led me to the lakeshore. Upon arriving back at the lodge I noticed that the skiff was gone. Only a few hours earlier I had asked Rick to take me for a boat ride, or go for a walk and he had declined. Now he was in the skiff in the lake. I put the spotting scope out on the deck and watched him as he rounded the face of Falcon Crest and back to the lodge.

He came inside he told me that he had heard shots fired while he was at the head of the lake. This is disturbing as there is not anything opened for hunting right now and it is troubling to know someone is out there and possibly poaching.

Rick knew that I was disappointed about missing out on the boat ride so he offered to take me out and he suggested that I learn to operate the skiff. I thought that was a good idea so off we went. We beached the skiff across the lake and walked around for a while. I was thrilled to find another eagle feather and I caught on to operating the skiff just fine.

11/8

The weather is good so we took the skiff out again. We cruised the east shore looking for life and the only things spotted were eagles, and plenty of them.

We beached the skiff at the creek and while Rick stood guard I walked the beach looking for treasures. I came across a very large set of bear tracks, which were big enough that I could fit my entire boot inside of the track without touching the outside edges of his print. I was excited and hoped to see that big boy, but not too close.

Continuing in the skiff we rounded the corner where I had been walking and two bears were approaching from the direction that I was headed. If I had gone around the corner we would have met face to face! That gave me an eerie feeling. When the bears saw and heard the skiff they took off running and went straight up a mountainside. Within seconds the two bears were out of sight.

A little farther up the beach we spotted a red fox running along the shore and Rick shot at it but missed. We were bobbing in the water. I cannot figure out what is his attraction is in shooting at things but I am thankful that he is a lousy shot. Then I considered he may not hit his target to protect us if the time came. I decided that I better start carrying my own rifle. I suggested that he do some target practice and the look he gave me told me that he did not like that comment very well.

As usual, we beached the skiff at the head of the lake and saw lots of bear and eagle tracks along the shore in the sand. One set of tracks was also very large and I think probably the same bear as we have in the past.

We discussed spending the night in the spike camp so beached the skiff to check supplies. The cabin was not stocked at all answering that question. We know what we need to bring the next time we came this direction. It is critical for the camps to be stocked.

We hiked up behind the cabin and sat on the hill enjoying the spectacular view.

Farther down the shore we came to another large covey of ptarmigan. I am surprised to see the amount of them this year. Again, they just sat still in the alders as we passed. I think that they think if they hold still that we will not see them.

11/9-10

A different falcon was spotted today. This one was quite large and after looking through the books we believe it to be a Peregrine.

This afternoon we heard Theo over the radio as he discussed plans to fly to Port Moller, so I baked a pie and prepared for company. Sure enough, the buzz of a plane could be heard so we were at the airstrip to greet the plane. Along with the mail and a nice visit he brought fresh fruit and vegetables.

23

Far Out

11/14/95

Days have passed and it has been cold and clear again so I could not stand staying indoors any longer. I bundled up and headed across the tundra behind dump hill. I came across several bear tracks that pointed to the head of the lake. I have not seen any bruins in awhile but I hope to see more of them before they hibernate. I also came across some ranger tracks, which gave me an idea of where we might be able to take the machine. I followed them for quite a distance as they worked their way back to and from the lodge. I am getting farther away from the lodge while out on my treks this year. I was thrilled to find an adult eagle feather at the Fish and Game cabin. It is always exciting for me.

It is cooling back down this evening and freezing things up.

11/15

It was a beautiful morning today so we took the ranger out and headed across the tundra. We worked our way through backwaters and the swamps. The ranger has opened up a new world of adventure for us. We were about four miles out when we spotted a single bear who had also spotted us. The big bear stood up on his hind legs trying to get a better look at us then went down on all fours and began running right at us! I looked back at the lodge, which was barely in sight, and my next thought was why did we go so far away from the safety of our shelter. We are vulnerable out here on the tundra. My stomach went up into my throat as I watched the brown ball of fur as he continued to run straight in our direction. Knowing that we had the rifle did not bring much comfort. I do not trust Rick's aim, he would probably only make it madder, and I do not want to shoot a bear anyway. This bear was really scaring me as it continued to run towards us coming close enough that we could see his powerful muscles work under his flowing fur coat with each movement that the giant burin made. The bear came within about 200 feet of us then stood up on his hind legs taking a good long look.

The exchange seemed like forever before the bear went back down on all fours then turned and ran off; heading back the same direction the bear had come from. It is possible that the bear may have had a fresh kill to protect, or perhaps just curious, then there are cubs, but in all cases, it was a huge relief that the situation did not end up in a conflict. I had wanted to see more bears this season, and I got a good look at this one.

Excitement finally over took fear and as we waited to move on until the bear was gone. I will never forget the feeling of thinking I am going to be attacked by a bear. It brought out emotions that I did not know I had. Rick asked if I wanted to go back to the lodge, but I said no, and we continued on.

We came across several frozen ponds and sat on top of a hill in the sun to enjoy the lunch that I had packed. With the present position of the sun we knew that we only had a few hours of daylight left so we began to work our way back to the lodge. We followed our tracks back and crossed the frozen water but all at once, we broke through the ice. The ranger went in the water with a sudden jolt, throwing us off. The water was hip deep and even though the engine was in the water it continued to run. While doing so, it was throwing water through the air and drenched us completely as we worked to get the monster machine out. The ice was thick making it difficult to break as we attempted to make a path. The ranger crawled a few inches at a time and at one point, it was all we could do to keep it from tipping over but fortunately for us, it did not.

We finally got it out of the water but it was still on the wrong side of the creek. We took it to a different location and held our breath as we crossed the ice, this time successfully.

11/17

The winds have been blowing and we have been tired and sore from our last excursion so we have spent a couple of days inside. The dogs did not even want to go out and would come right back to the door quickly after letting them out in the morning.

I was eating a sugar daddy and my front crown came off of all things. I radioed Arlene to see if there was a dentist in the neighborhood, ha ha, but of course out here, there is not. I was told however, that I was in luck as a dentist would be coming to Nelson Lagoon at the end of the month so I would only have to wait until then. Theo said that he would fly over and get me so even though it looks bad, I talk funny, and it hurts slightly, I am in pretty good shape.

11/18

In talking with several people in Nelson Lagoon the subject of ptarmigan came up and they stated how much they would love to have some. They said that they did not have the opportunity to get ptarmigan without coming over this direction, so we decided to try and get some birds for them. We took the skiff out and just like one might expect, did not see any.

When we did not have intentions of hunting them we saw thousands of them and now that we want to hunt them, we cannot find any.

After the boat ride, I went for a walk along the backwaters and followed several sets of bear tracks. It is nice to know that animals are still around. The critters must be passing at night, as we are not seeing them. I found a spot in the mud where a bear had laid down and rolled. A mud bath I figure. I followed the tracks to the Fish and Game cabin and looked at all of the damage that the bears are doing to the building. The bruins are biting and tearing the molding and siding off, leaving splintered wood lying everywhere. I went in the cabin to see if food or something was left which could be attracting them and it is a bit scary in there. I wondered if I was brave enough to spend the night in the cabin.

11/19

The day was spent ptarmigan hunting again. This time we got three ptarmigan and Parti-girl did her job of locating the downed birds for us. Parti-girl is a great hunting partner. Rick walked the hillside and got two birds and I shot one from the skiff.

11/20

I was restless and tried to get Rick to go out in the skiff but he was not interested. He kept suggesting that I go by myself and at times my stubborn nature takes over common since, which it did today. I was irritated that he would not go so I gathered my daypack a rifle and headed out in the skiff with the dogs.

I went across the lake and worked my way up the east shore while I searched for wildlife. I planned to go around the lake and for a while I was very proud of myself.

That all changed when the wind suddenly kicked up from the south making the water very rough. I was near the head of the lake as white caps began to crest all around me. I was afraid to turn the skiff around not wanting to get the boat sideways in the waves fearing it would be swamped and capsize. I did not know what to do. What a fine mess I have gotten myself into this time, I thought.

The skiff was being tossed around throwing the dogs off of the benches and onto the floor. They were struggling to keep their footing and did not like it, so they came to the back of the skiff to be by me for comfort and reassurance. This caused more problems with the weight of the dogs transferred to the back of the skiff causing the bow came up and the stern down allowing water to splash inside the skiff from the rear. It was difficult to keep the skiff heading in a straight direction while attempting to convince the dogs to settle in on the floor. Once I got the dogs settled, I stayed as close to the shore as possible aware of how deep the lake is on the east shore. I was aware that if the skiff went down we were in serious trouble.

The wind blew harder and the waves got bigger churning in all directions tossing and slamming the boat on the water. I knew, somehow, I had to turn back. It was a different kind of fear that I had experienced when the bear charged at us out on the tundra but I was scared.

Feeling like I had no choice, I made the move and turned the skiff. It bobbed in the water as the waves splashed over the sides just as I had feared. I cannot say why or how, but we got turned around and even though the waves were splashing against the stern and drenching me, we were heading away from the rough water and back towards the lodge.

I worked our way down the shoreline and was so relieved when we finally out ran the storm gliding through calm waters once again. The sick feeling left from me and I have never been so thankful.

Just across from the lodge I spotted several ptarmigan in the alders so I beached the skiff and headed out after them. It was a good excuse to get out of the boat; it felt good to be on dry land. I continued to follow the ptarmigan while they continued to fly ahead of me. They would not fly very far. I did get off a couple of rounds and added four more birds to the ptarmigan that we already had.

I laid in bed this evening and shuttered at the days experience. It was a lesson well learned.

24

Return to Lagoon

11/23/95

The last few days have been spent inside working on Christmas gifts. Theo radioed that he would be up to get me on Friday, weather permitting of course. Little Allen also radioed and asked me if I wanted to go glass float hunting again. Of course I said yes and I am excited about everything. I drifted off to sleep as I watched several shooting stars race across the sky.

I am packed and ready to go but a storm came in instead of Theo. Weather conditions dictate activities and I have learned to accept that. Maybe the weather will be nice tomorrow.

I spent the day playing with the keyboards while Rick re-plumbed the fuel lines that feed diesel into the generator. The fuel lines have frozen twice shutting the heat off but his efforts will hopefully solve that problem. After watching the Princess Di interview, which I enjoyed, we played trivial pursuit. All of a sudden, without saying a word Rick got up and went upstairs and did not come back. I guess that would be a forfeit.

11/26

It was a calm and clear day this morning and before I was even dressed I heard the buzz of the Theo's plane. I rushed upstairs, took a quick shower changing from my usual attire of sweat pants and shirt.

This is my first time flying with Theo and before we took off he explained where the first aid kit and other emergency gear are located in the plane. That impressed me, as he was the first bush pilot that I had flown with to take the time to do that. He had a second set of headgear that he handed to me to wear. I was able to hear him talk to the tower in Cold Bay as he confirmed his flight plans. That was really cool and it also made it much easier for us to talk over the loud and awesome sound of the airplane engine. He flew a lot closer to the ground than I was use to and flew me by Herendeen Bay to show me Allen's grave. From there we went to Nelson Lagoon and as we circled the airstrip along the Bearing Sea, I was thrilled to see a pod of Orcas whales! There were many of them ranging in all sizes. The bulls have large dorsal fins that stood high and proud as the calves showed their playful nature while they swim. It was awesome to watch as they rose out of the water and dipped back into the sea. Theo flew an extra circle to allow me the view. The Orcas were heading north. I could have watched all night, but we descended and touched down, ending a perfect flight.

I am also impressed at the sight of the huge dock that was built here last summer. It is in the mouth of the river and opens up a whole new world of shopping and shipping for the residents of the village.

After landing I helped Theo secure the plane then he drove me to Arlene's house where I will be staying. Dailey and Sharon came over to visit and invited me to stay at their homes but I wanted to stay with Arlene. After losing Allen it was something I needed to do as well as I know that she could use the company and support.

Several people came to visit this evening and I enjoy seeing the familiar faces as well as, meeting a few new ones. Arlene made ptarmigan soup and I will admit it was good.

11/28
The tides have made it very difficult to get out on the beach as the water has been very rough and the low tides are after dark. I was able to get out for one nice walk but did not find much. The high and rough waters have cleaned the beach. Arlene took me down the beach in her 4-runner but we did not spot a single float. We laughed as she drove furious and fast up the beach to beat the waves that pounded on the shores while the tide came in.

11/29-29

Today the dentist arrived at the village and set up for patients. They fit me in and I was thankful to have my crown cemented back in place. No more sugar daddies for me. The dentist and his assistant are from Anchorage. They are part of a team who are flown in to several different villages throughout the year. The service is free to the natives and they did not charge me either.

The evenings have been very enjoyable spending them at Arlene's with many other village residents. We play guitars and sing until early morning; in fact it was 5:30 before we retired this morning. I counted 28 people in and out of the house tonight. That is half of the winter population in this village. I admire how close these people are, they are loving and supportive of each other.

It is a beautiful day today and Merlin and Breezy kept bugging Theo to take them flying. He finally gave in to their continuing harassment and bribes and I was thrilled when I was invited to fly along. Theo seated Merlin and Breezy in the back seats allowing me to sit second seat.

We flew down the coastline and spotted a caribou herd. From there we flew over the villages' water source, the large, fresh water pond, they call Water Lake, then over to Maxi's summer camp on the river. His camp is a large house built on the banks of the river. I would love to spend a season camping there. The camp is only accessible by boat or small plane.

We continued to fly along the river and I spotted several other camps. Some camps are still being used while others are old and abandoned. It is intriguing to try to imagine what life would have been like for the people here in the early days, as well as life today. I do know that it is very challenging and I respect the families who endure this life as it is a lot of hard work.

As we continued, I stayed glued to the windows absorbed in the sights. Theo asked me, over the headphone mic, if I was ready to fly. Being the senseless person that I tend to be, with great excitement I said, "Sure!" The Cessna has two sets of controls allowing either person in the front seats access to the controls of the plane. Theo had me put my hands on my controls while he maneuvered the plane allowing me to get a feel of flying this plane while he explained some things such as, the difference between slicing and flying.

When he felt that I was ready he turned the plane over to me, which was way beyond thrilling! Becoming a pilot has been a dream of mine for many years and this felt fantastic! Theo told me to follow the winding river below and turned around to talk with the guys. It was great to see their reactions when they realized Theo was no longer flying the plane, but I was. Their expressions were priceless! Theo pointed out the location where Allen had drowned and as we passed over we all sat in silence. From there, we continued along the river over the mouth of the bay and circled for a landing. Of course the control was given back to the real pilot for that. Once again, a perfect landing and we were back on solid ground.

Arlene and I decided to spend the night at the fox den and began making preparations. We tried to sneak away to spend the time as a getaway for her but there are no secrets in the village and throughout the evening the vehicles continued to arrive at the den. It was fun anyway and the last of the gang pulled out around midnight.

Arlene Nelson

Maxi Johnson & Little Alan

Dailey and brother, Jack

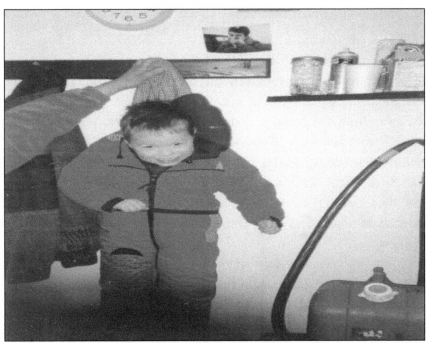

Another term for "Hanging" in Nelson Lagoon

Everyone left except Merlin and Breezy. Arlene took claim to the bottom bunk, told the guys that I get the top and if they wanted to stay they would have to sleep on the floor, which is what they did.

It got way too hot on the top bunk and I was having trouble standing it so around 3 am I went out on the porch to cool off. The wind was blowing hard and the air felt great. I decided not to go back inside and instead got into Arlene's rig to sleep the rest of the night. The wind blew so hard that the vehicle swayed and bobbed as the air whistled through the gaps. I did not sleep but enjoyed the storm.

Arlene came out around 8 am, in a panic, when she realized that I was not in my bunk. Arlene stated it was dark when she woke up and did not want to disturb the rest of us while we slept so she sat quietly at the table waiting.

As the light came, in Arlene looked at my bunk realizing that I was not there, feared that I had decided to attempt to walk back to the village or something crazy like that. We had a big laugh out of it once she found me.

12/1

The morning was nice, we had breakfast as we waited for the tide to cooperate and allow us out on the beach. Instead of heading straight home we drove even farther south. Arlene took a road that led away from the ocean and drove to Water Lake. While we were there, Prebin and John Jr. showed up in a vehicle, we talked for a few minutes but because of the incoming tide, we needed to make a mad dash back up the beach to the village. Several times the waves came in real high causing us to swerve drastically to dodge them. We all laughed as none of us have any sense I guess! Once again, life was thrilling.

The last evening was spent at Arlene's house enjoying the company of many members of the village. We were entertained with a home video that Maxi brought over to play. They have all watched it or were there when the event occurred but never get tired of watching it again. It was filmed last fishing season when a brown bear swam out in the river and climbed onto a fishing boat that was anchored to a buoy. It was amazing as we watched the bear pull himself out of the water and over the side of the boat with little effort. Fortunately no one was on the boat at the time. The bear snooped around and went into the galley and tore up the cabin making a huge mess of things. Seal bombs were being thrown onto the boat in an effort to scare the bear off of the boat but the bear ignored them. When the bear was ready, the bear crawled over the side of the boat getting back into the water and swam to shore. Bears are truly remarkable animals.

12/2

This morning we woke to heavy winds appearing that we would not be able to fly, but as the day wore on the winds subsided so Theo and I loaded the plane and headed back to the lodge. We stopped at Port Moller to get mail then followed Bear River back to the lake.

Several letters and packages arrived for us including a package from Norway, via the wanderers. It contained Norwegian chocolate. Heaven in a wrapper!

I made a comment about Swedish chocolate which caused Lars and Marit to immediately defend the chocolate from their county, Norway, stating their chocolate was better than Swiss chocolate. I indicated that I would need to be the judge of that so they had some chocolate sent to me. The chocolate is very rich, creamy, and melted in my mouth. I am now ruined for American chocolate.

25

December Arrives

12/3/95

I spent most of the day putting up Christmas decorations and getting ready for Christmas. I am trying to limit my sweet intake this year as I gained about thirty pounds last winter here and sure do not want to do that again. This time of year makes that rough for me as I have traditional items that I make for the holidays.

12/4

Today was spent writing Christmas cards. I am glad to be back at the lodge but I do feel alone especially after being with wonderful people. I thrive on the quiet, peaceful life here so I am a bit torn right now.

The temperatures have been low again and there is a fresh layer of snow. Without saying anything Rick went out for a walk across the tundra. I spotted him in the scope as he worked his way back towards the lodge. A large pit grew in my stomach when I also spotted a good-sized bear tracking and following behind him. It did not look like Rick was aware of the bear behind him and as I watched I wondered if I was going to see Rick mauled. I tried calling him over the radio but after several attempts he either could not hear me or the hand held radio is turned off. Watching through the scope it is hard to tell the depth of field so I was not sure how close the bear actually was to him but it was obviously tracking him. I continued to watch and was relieved when Rick crossed the back waters at dump hill while the bear turned and headed up lake. I went outside to greet him and told him about the bear and Rick confirmed that he had no idea. He never once turned around and looked behind him. His face turned pale as I spoke.

12/5-6

It got down to three degrees last night and the temperature only rose to seventeen during the day. Because of previous problems with freezing fuel lines, we decided that any time the temperature gets ten or below we will leave the generator running. It is much easier to keep things flowing than it is to thaw things out. Around midnight the lines froze anyway and everything shut down and went quiet. Rick went out and took the necessary measures to un-thaw the lines and get the power back on.

In the light of the full moon Rick has been putting bait out on the beach in front of the lounge and watching most of the night in hopes that something would come along, but to my delight, so far, no takers.

I woke up again around 5 am to a very cold room as the fuel lines have once again frozen up that feed the heater. I went outside and poured hot water over them thawing them but my efforts did not last long before the pipes were frozen and the heater stopped burning again. Along with more hot water and the sun that had raised the pipes finally flowed free.

I spent the rest of the day preparing Christmas packages for mailing out.

12/8

The wind has shifted and is now blowing from the south bringing in warmer temperatures and a reprieve for all concerns. Pat radioed and said that he had been out on the beach and came across a dead bear. It was lying in an area that they call Frank's Lagoon. Talking to Pat inspired me to go out for a walk.

It felt good to get some fresh air and in my walk I found two eagle feathers. Rick spent most of the day building a raft. The waters in the river have lowered to a point that going down river in the skiff is out of the question and he is determined to go down stream. He might get down river alright, but I wonder how he intends to get back. That will be one adventure I will turn down even if I am invited.

12/9

I have felt the need to be outside lately so today I put the chest waders on and crossed the river to take a walk on the wild side. I found one eagle feather, two traps and bones, bones, and more bones.

I followed a trail of bones, which led me to the skull and antlers of a young caribou. I was surprised at the number of fresh fox dens that are in the area. It looks like an apartment complex on Bear Hill. I returned to the lodge only to discover that the lines feeding the heater had frozen up again. I used hot water to get the fuel running then gathered supplies and wrapped and taped insulation around the lines.

12/10

I had strange dreams last night about sick pet elephants and attacking bears that had gotten inside my truck. As crazy as it sounds it spooked me all day and I waited for Rick to get up and go out to start the generator this morning.

It has snowed through the night and as the afternoon wore on I decided to be brave and face my fears by going outside for a short walk. I went down to the Fish and Game cabin then back to the lodge following the backwaters. No sign of life today.

I decided to fish for a while and immediately caught three silver salmon, which were all released. They are pretty dark in color now but even if they were not, I enjoy watching them swim away as I place them back in the river instead of keeping them. After catching three so fast, I turned the fishing into a game of trying to cast my lure out in the river and retrieve it without catching a fish. When I would see a fish going for the lure I would jerk my line to try and avoid catching the fish. I still caught a few more and laughed, as I never thought that I would see that day.

2/11

This morning I was feeling braver so with a flashlight in hand I went out to start the generator. I noticed Cowboy sniffing the ground and following the scent of something. All at once he let out a few yelps and the race was on! It was a relief to see that Cowboy was in pursuit of a fox and I laughed as Parti-girl and her slow self, joined in on the chase. I was amused while I stood and watched as the two dogs teamed up and chased the fox around and around the lodge building. It was comedy at its finest. At one point the fox and Cowboy lapped poor Parti-girl. As usual, the fox eventually ditched them. The dogs ran around lost; trying to figure out where the sly fox had gone and in the process discovered something of great interest under the guest building.

I took the flashlight and got down on my hands and knees to take a look for myself only to discover a porcupine. Both dogs were under the building as well and neither of them would call off as they barked and harassed the quilled enemy. Cowboy finally gave up but Parti-girl did not stop while the morning wore on. When she did finally grow quiet she showed up with quills in her face. Rick got up annoyed by the noise and went out and shot the porcupine.

Next we had to deal with the quills in her face. After that chore was done Rick made a loop on a pole and pulled the intruder out from under the building and took it across the river laying it on the beach. The birds came immediately for the free meal. I watched as the birds worked at the porcupine. They were very careful as they pulled at the meat from the belly so that they could avoid the quills.

12/12

Rick put his raft in the river today and even though it was floating, bubbles were coming from one of the barrels that he had used for floatation so he pulled it back out of the river and proceeded to take it apart to change the barrel. He is serious about his intentions of going downstream and I am uncomfortable about it. At this point, I am not just concerned about him placing himself in jeopardy, but also the fact that he is putting us all in jeopardy.

12/13

Another December 13 has arrived; this year is my 41st birthday. I woke to a fresh snowfall and enjoyed the wonderful birthday given to me. Rick asked me if I wanted to go for a boat ride but before I could get ready, fog came in so it was just as well that we did not go.

I walked down to the Fish and Game cabin and found several areas where wolf prints are very heavy. There are many sets of them and one set of tracks is extremely large. Because of the fresh snow I knew that they had to have been there last night or this morning so I followed the tracks as they worked their way down river for about two miles. It was interesting to observe their habits. Knowing that the tracks were probably only a few hours old was also very exciting. I never did spot the wolves but that is ok as I did not need a dog wolf issue.

I did find one eagle feather and came across a lot of other animal tracks including, fox, beaver, and mink. I am amazed at how alive this place really is, as at times it appears so lifeless.

The river is very low and in places only ankle deep. I must have seen at least one hundred eagles today. They were everywhere. I kept the secret of the wolves to myself and enjoyed the day immensely as we topped it off with halibut fish and chips. I was very touched at the many radio calls that I received from members of the village as they wished me happy birthday. We drank a bottle of champagne and lit fireworks off of the deck, which has become a tradition for special events. Rick got the idea to put a message in the champagne bottle and we launched it downstream. We posted our names, location, and address on the note asking that if someone found it to please write us. I had a good day.

12/14

Today started out foggy but cleared off and we both went for a long walk down river. We walked about four miles down and followed game trails up on Moller Hill. I was thrilled to be able to see the ocean from the top of the hills and yearned to get out on the beach again.

There were wolf tracks everywhere so the secret is out. Once again, no wolves were spotted but now that Rick knows that they are around, he will be watching for them. Parti-girl found a frozen pond that had a beaver moving around in the water under the ice and she followed it on top of the ice attempting to get at it for a long time. She ran back and forth across the pond until the ice broke and she fell through. After several failed attempts to get herself out, Rick pulled her to safety. We could hear the beaver grunting at us from under the ice. Beavers make really strange noises.

We also saw a porcupine and some ptarmigan. The ptarmigan are completely white now and unless they move they are hard to spot. We were tired and glad to be back at the lodge and as I sat there looking out the window I noticed a little ermine running around in the yard. He is white with a dark tip on his tail and is a very busy little boy! It was entertaining as he ran back and forth, ducking and darting.

12/15

The day was a rough one, as Rick got very drunk early in the day. He passed out on the floor for several hours then got up and went upstairs to sleep it off. I radioed to Nelson Lagoon attempting to locate Theo to ask him to come and get me, but found out that his was in King Cove, visiting with family. Rick got back up late in the afternoon and began drinking again and this time we got into a huge argument over it. Needing to clear my head I bundled up and went out for a long walk up the lake beach. Before I returned back at the lodge it had gotten dark and I was fairly nervous as well as the walking was challenging. I came across some bear tracks in the sand that had not been there on my way out and some very weird sensations over took me. I was hoping that Rick would come looking for me but he did not. I had not taken a rifle with me either. I finally made it back to the lodge only to find him still passed out in the same position he was in when I left. He did not even know that I had been gone. I cannot blame him for my leaving and I will not do that again, I hope.

12/17

I have started watching home instruction tapes for getting a pilot's license and I am enjoying it. The information is very interesting to me and the distraction is good. Nothing stirring, just me.

It is very windy and rainy outside so I spent the day watching and studying flying. Theo is planning to come in the first fly day and pick up our outgoing Christmas mail but as the holiday draws closer and the storms continue, it is not looking good that they will arrive in time for Christmas. Oh well, just another thing that is to be expected with life in the bush.

12/18

The storm has finally passed allowing a plane to fly in. Theo brought fresh produce and took the packages and outgoing mail. I did not mention anything about going. He did not stop in Port Moller to get our incoming mail but that does not bother me, as I was just relieved to get the mail out. He also brought Jack with him today and as always, it was wonderful to see and talk to people. We always hope they can stay longer but as we were visiting, a radio call came in from Nelson Lagoon stating that the fog was setting in there and they either needed to stay, or get on their way. As tradition, I stood at the edge of the airstrip while the plane lifted and flew into the distance, wondering what stopped me from getting on the plane with them.

12/19

It was very nice and I wanted to go out in the boat but Rick did not feel like going so instead I put on chest waders and crossed the river to go for a walk. I had told a few people about my experience of going out in the skiff alone and they were mad that Rick would suggest such a dangerous thing and scolded me for doing it making it clear not to do that again. They really did not need to worry about that. I would not ever be out in the boat alone again.

I was happy to walk and I followed the game trails along the top of Bear Hill. The dogs got a long way ahead of me and began barking like crazy. When I caught up to them my suspicions were confirmed. Cowboy found his enemy, another porcupine. I am surprised and not too thrilled at the amount of porcupines out here. Cowboy also had a few quills in his face so I headed back to the lodge to take care of him. He is so stubborn and it appears that now he has a strong vengeance towards them and wants to win, not understanding that he cannot win.

On the trek back I found one eagle feather from an immature eagle. It is beautiful with the marbling of brown and white. These feathers are my favorite.

As I crossed the river back to the lodge I was really upset to discover Rick preparing the skiff for a ride. I do not understand and let him go without speaking to him.

Cowboy and I went inside to the grueling task of removing the quills. Rick came back a short time later and asked if I wanted to go for a ride. Even though I was mad at him, I am not so stubborn to let that get in the way of an adventure, so off we went. This time, I carried my own rifle.

We beached the skiff at the creek across the lake and walked around spotting lots of bear, wolf, fox, and eagle tracks but other than the eagles, we did not see anything. The tracks are not fresh as the ground is frozen and hard. Our own footsteps did not even leave tracks in the sand. We rounded the head of the lake and it was really cold. The salmon are still active in the headwaters, which surprised me. I was excited to see the amount of eagles that we spotted at cabin hill and once back at the lodge I took my waders off only to discover that they had leaked and my pants were damp.

12/20

We built a fire in the sauna for the first time and enjoyed the heat of it. I do not know what madness got into me as I ran out naked and flung myself into the icy cold Bear River. I guess it was something that I had to try, at least once, and it will be the last. It was a horrible idea. The water stung my skin and my head hurt as I forced myself under. The one thing that did feel good once I got out of the water was the air felt warm. I spent some time walking the shore looking for treasures and laughed as I pictured someone flying in, or over and spotting me as I walked around naked. They would have hauled me out of here for sure.

Snow started falling this evening and I am hoping that it will hold through Christmas.

12/21

Rick spent last night preparing for his trip down river stating that he is going to take his raft and go to Port Moller. I cannot even imagine what he is thinking as he knows that is not even possible.

We have been to the mouth of the river and it is very dangerous but I did not say anything as he announced his plans. He sat around all morning trying to decide whether to go or not and to my surprise he did take off but not in the raft, in the skiff. He gave up on the idea of taking the raft even though he had seen from our last walk down stream that the river is very low in many places. The cloud cover is also low and visibility is bad. I cannot believe that he is doing this.

I watched from the lounge as he worked his way downstream. When he got too far away to see well, I set up the spotting scope and continued to follow his movements hoping to see him turn back. He spent more time out of the skiff dragging it than he floated. Even though he had the hand held radio I did not hear from him until late this evening. He is at the cabin down river and was held up there.

My first night alone in the lodge was a bit strange and I found myself waking often through the night. Even though the two dogs were with me, the lodge was very quiet and felt empty. I did my favorite things like making fudge and studying the flying manual to help pass the time but in the back of my mind all I could think about was wondering if I would see Rick alive again. The weather the last few days has been pretty poor with the conditions changing back and forth rapidly. One minute it is clear and the next minute it is so foggy that you cannot see.

12/22

I have been leaving the main generator running and do not get very far from the radio. The only time I am away from it is when I am in the lounge with the scope while I scan the empty tundra. Some relief did come when Rick finally made a radio call. He stayed at the cabin and has decided to turn back.

I spent the rest of the day watching for him in the scope. It got dark and he had not arrived but he finally radioed again to say that he had to go back to the cabin because of the low waters and would attempt walking back to the lodge the next day. I suggested that he just stay there and wait for spring when the water levels would raise enough for him to bring the skiff back. The conversation ended abruptly and I did not hear back from him.

12/23

I did spend much of the day in the lounge looking through the spotting scope and late afternoon I spotted Rick walking towards the lodge. I bundled up and walked out to meet him. He said that he secured the skiff and as soon as the river rises, he would go back and get it.

I was glad that he was safe, but not very happy about the risk that he took. As we crossed the backwaters of the lodge we spotted a fox, which was out hunting for dinner. He found a shrew in the bank and would crouch like a cat and spring at his prey until he finally succeeded. He was so involved at what he was doing that he did not notice us pass by. I continued watching him from inside the lodge as he eventually worked his way into the yard only to be greeted by the dogs and the chase was on. Round and round the lodge they went. I think it is the same fox that has played this game with them before. Cowboy yelped the entire time. The fox finally got tired of the game and headed up the beach of the lake with both dogs running behind it. Neither dog showed back up for a couple of hours and both of them were worn out. Guess we will all get some sleep tonight.

12/24

It is now Christmas Eve and I was restless today so decided to go out and see if the fish were still active. I was surprised to catch four Dolly Varden and eight silver salmon. I released them all. A couple more fish that I hooked got themselves off before I reeled them in and the last one that I hooked got away with my pixie so I called it a good day of fishing.

Throughout the day, several people from Nelson Lagoon radioed to wish us a Merry Christmas and as always, it meant so much. I radioed back a Christmas wish to the entire village and the rest of the evening Christmas songs and jokes were shared over the radio. The people of Nelson Lagoon were in fine spirits and it was entertaining listening to them.

12/25

We woke this morning with warm temperatures and only patches of snow left on the ground. I was thankful for that counting it a white Christmas.

I talked to my family via the radio and that helped my day. The family said that the packages did not arrive but the cards did so even though I was disappointed, they should arrive soon. Most of the day was spent, on my part anyway, preparing for a holiday meal.

12/26

Today is another warm day. I have been working on a military jacket for a friend of ours who lives in Kenai. The ribbing has frayed on the cuffs and waistband and he offered to pay me to try and fix it. I have no intention of charging him, I am happy to help even though it turned into a much bigger chore than I had expected. I knew that the leather jacket and his time served in Viet Nam meant a great deal to him.

12/27

The wind blew all night with gusts as high as 71 mph. Things settled by the afternoon so I went out for a walk up the lake beach, over the hill, along the backwaters, and down to the Fish and Game cabin. I went inside the cabin and sat there for quite some time.

I was back in the lodge when Little Allen radioed and we had a nice visit. I sure appreciate the people of Nelson Lagoon though I doubt that they have any idea how much they help me while I attempt to stay sane.

12/28

Today was exciting when I heard the plans over the radio concerning Theo flying in. I prepared for company and was very happy when he landed with Leona in the plane with him. She is spending the winter in Anchorage taking flying lessons and I have missed not spending time with her so far this winter. She was home for the holidays and we had a fun visit. All we could talk about was flying and they were surprised by how much I have learned. As always, their time here seemed too short.

The evening was enjoyed while the mail was opened and read.

12/29

Today was another nice day so I went out feather hunting. I had a great walk but no feathers. The river is rising and I am keeping an eye on it hoping that we can get downriver to retrieve the skiff. I crossed the river several times to cut corners and had trouble with the depths and the current. I was following tracks along backwaters and got into some mud that was challenging because each step I took I was sinking deeper. The mud was above my knees and pulling at my boots making every step difficult. I had the rifle with me and did not want to get it in the mud, which made things even harder. It took quite some time and most of my energy to get out of the mess so when I was once again on steady ground I headed back to the lodge.

As I cut across the tundra I noticed a bright orange object in the distance so I walked over to it discovering a rubber-fishing buoy, with bear teeth marks in it.

Bears like toys and are curious. As I examined it I wished that I had been able to watch the bear with the buoy. The lodge is about 15 miles away from the ocean. I carried the buoy back to the lodge, happy with my latest treasure.

When I came to the backwaters behind the dump I was nervous to cross the ice because of the warm temperatures that we have been having so I sat on the bank for a while and watched the dogs on the ice before choosing my spot to cross. The ice was scary as it was clear and I could see the water rushing under the ice and the water is fairly deep. I held my breath as I took each step successfully crossing without incident. On the lodge side I spotted a large group of sea gull feathers lying on the ground. It was obvious that one of the falcons had hit it with their enormous force exploding it in the air. The bird itself was cleaned up completely. Nothing goes to waste out here. As I approached the lodge I felt good for the outing and spent the rest of the day watching for the falcon or anything else that moved, but saw nothing.

12/30

This evening Pat radioed and told us that Theo was in Cold Bay and took a list of items from us to be picked up while he was there. It was just like shopping.

12/31

Another New Years Eve is upon us and the last day of the year closed with a windy, rainy, storm that rushed through this evening. Out like a lion and in like a lamb. I continue to be amazed at how quickly things change around here. We had a nice dinner complete with champagne and then fireworks.

26

Another New Year

1/1/95

New Years day was rainy and windy so I spent most of the day studying ground school flight information. We spoke to several people in Nelson Lagoon as we exchanged New Years greetings.

1/2

I have stayed in for a few days both because of the crummy weather and also because I am absorbed in the information that I am studying on flying. I am enjoying what I am learning and have found that I am fascinated with the maps. The first time that I looked at an aeronautical chart I thought it was a waste of paper and ink, certainly not of much assistance, but after understanding what I was looking at, I find them loaded with valuable and necessary information.

1/3-4

I finally forced myself to get out and go for a walk. I needed the break and the fresh air. It really felt great. Birds are the only sign of life.

Leona radioed to say good-bye as she is returning to Anchorage to finish her flying school. I am excited and envious of her for that. It will take me much longer.

1/6

The moon is full so the dogs are not sleeping well, which means either am I, but time means nothing here. I have never experienced that kind of freedom before and I like the lifestyle.

1/7

Last night the dogs kept disturbing me so around 3 am I got up and just sat at the window enjoying the sights across the land under the light of the moon. When I did finally fall back to sleep I dreamt of earthquakes and erupting volcanoes. Feeling the strength of such powerful forces is quite remarkable. It was educating and in some ways fascinating to experience the events, without really living it.

I took the Christmas decorations down today and the rooms feel so empty and bare. It will take a few days to get use to evenings without the wonderful little lights. We went for a short walk this afternoon and as always, it felt good to get out.

1/10

Not too much exciting lately except for the new snow and low temperatures again. The wind chill has the temperatures down to minus 76! The actual temperature ranged from zero to 6 above. I went out for a walk and took some pictures. It is awesome out there. The cold sucks your breath away and I had to keep my face and mouth covered to breathe. The only part of my body that was exposed was my eyes and at times they were closed. I needed goggles. It was great but only because I knew that I had a warm shelter to go back to.

It seems like every day something is freezing and we are struggling to keep the heater and generator running, as well as the water pipes draining. The generator froze up three times today. I think that Warren should spend a winter out here. I realize that dealing with the lodge is our responsibility but with a little effort; many of the hardships might not exist.

1/11

The sun finally came out today and I really love how the snow glitters against the light. The extreme beauty makes me feel so good. Jack radioed from Nelson Lagoon to say hi. He said that Theo is hoping to fly in on Saturday. That was good news and something to look forward to.

1/13

Saturday arrived and so did the plane bringing our mail and supplies we ordered. We are still receiving Christmas presents. Having visitors was great but other than that, it has been pretty quiet around here. The wind has shifted and blowing from the south again which has been a good reprieve for the animals and equipment.

1/14

Today something else is wrong with the generator and if it were not for going out to deal with it several times I would not have gotten out at all. I heard a plane fly overhead and went out and stood on the porch just to listen. I could not see the plane as it was above the cloud cover. We heard over the radio that the plane was going to Sand Point. Just hearing it was a link with the outside world. I chuckled as I thought about the people in the plane had no idea someone was down on the ground looking for life to have a connection with.

1/18

I went out for a walk up the lake beach and enjoyed seeing the ice patterns that are forming along the water's edge.

The fox and bird tracks show a lot of activity out here and the snow has a real strange texture to it. The snow feels gritty, like sand. I have never felt snow like this before. It will not stick together.

The dogs allowed themselves to get pretty far ahead of me and when they were out of sight I ducked into the alders to play a game of hide and seek. I was curious to see how long it would take them to begin looking for me. Parti-girl was the first dog that noticed I was not in sight and came looking for me. I watched her sniff and follow my tracks as she ran straight to me. Cowboy did not turn back and I watched him run up the hill and disappear. I sat still hiding and waiting until I noticed that he was above me on the hill looking down and watching my every move as I waited. I am definitely no match in trying to out-wit the dogs.

1/19

Several mornings when I go out to start the generator I shine the flashlight across the lake and I see sets of eyes staring back at me. I am pretty sure that they are fox but it is still very eerie. My routine is to step off of the porch into the open area, then stand still as I shine my light around attempting to catch the glow of any eyes or movement so that I will be aware if something is there. The mornings that the dogs take off running and barking make me nervous. The dogs definitely are a good look out for me.

1/20

It has been pretty warm lately and there is standing water everywhere. At times it feels like spring. The birds are active in the mornings and it is nice to wake up to. As the day wore on, the force of extreme nature dictated what the day had in store for us all and by this evening the change brought wind, cool temperatures, and frozen rain.

1/23

The ground and waters still seem to be fairly frozen so we took a walk out across the tundra. Ice is allowing us to get farther than we have had access to before.

Many of the backwaters are frozen and the falls are spectacular as they froze in place. I do not think a camera could capture the picture that is planted forever in my mind. Some of the walking challenges today happened when my footsteps broke through the crust of the snow jolting my hips.

It is always exciting to cross the ice. It was especially challenging to walk on the ice where the water level has dropped below the ice level creating dead space. After we crossed frozen Milky River, we sat on the hillside and ate the lunch we had packed. It was time to turn back as we were a long distance from the lodge. Figuring it was approximately six miles out and knowing we have to walk back the same distance made me tired.

While making our return to the lodge a plane flew overhead at a low altitude. We could see their faces. We waved as it passed and learned later from Pat that it was Fish and Game out counting caribou. They stopped at Port Moller and talked with him.

We finally reached the lodge and I was pretty sore and tired. So were the dogs, they go at least twice as far running back and forth.

1/24

It has been snowing again lately. Not a lot but enough to cover the old tracks making everything fresh again. I did a little fishing and I am surprised to still be catching silvers this late as February is just around the corner. The salmon are very disgusting looking, hook mouths, open sores on their flesh and I stopped when it dawned on me that just catching them could take the last of what energy they had left.

1/26

Once again the wind has changed direction and is bringing in warm temperatures melting the snow. I went for a walk to the Fish and Game cabin and around the backwaters. The creeks are raging fast resulting in the ground being soft and muddy. I was very excited to find three small eagle feathers. Pat radioed and bet me five dollars on the Super Bowl game.

1/28

The Super Bowl is today and it was fun to radio Pat back stating the Cowboys rule and he owes me money.

1/31

Theo flew in early this morning. It was exciting to the buzz of his plane engine approaching. A lot of mail came in this delivery and we enjoyed the many letters that were received. Little Allen came with Theo and liked the leather baby moccasins that I have been making and wanted to buy a pair for a young nephew. I would not name a price so he told me he would get me some glass floats to trade. They said that some the people from Nelson Lagoon want me to come back over for another party, I mean visit so I plan to fly back with Theo the next time he flies in, maybe.

2/1

February came in with a boom bringing more snow and cold temperatures. I have been busy answering letters and studying flying tapes. I take the practice tests over and over to really implant the information in my mind.

2/2

It was a nice day today so I crossed the river and went for a walk up Bear Hill then cut out across the tundra. The dogs went straight to the porcupine again which was in the same location that they found him the last time. No quills today and I am very relieved for that. Walking is difficult across the rough and uneven tundra and I could not imagine walking any great distance out here.

2/3

I awoke today at 8:30 am and it was light enough to go outside to start the generator without a flashlight. It was great! I watched Bear Hill through the spotting scope and it was alive with fox. I am amazed how many fox are there and how busy they are. There is an entire fox community on the hillside, until the bears come back.

2/4

It has been cold the last several nights so the generator was left running. The temperature did not rise above ten degrees and the wind is blowing bringing the chill factor down to minus twenty-five. I have not gone outside much the last couple of days so I made a jump rope from leaded fish net rope and have been using that for exercise. With the lead weight in the rope I discovered in a hurry that you bring your legs quite high while jumping. I turn music on and jump to the rhythm.

27

Challenges

2/6/96

The weather has been awesome. It is still storming! The latest problem is the satellite dish is not moving properly or hardy at all. As soon as it got light I went out to take a look at it. I discovered that there is a stack of lumber that had been tossed on the ground and on top of the TV cable. The cable should have been buried anyway but over time, the movement of the dish has caused the cable to tighten and pulled the wires loose form the connection at the dish. I found the satellite manual and tried re-hooking it back by the diagrams but that is not working. I made many different attempts then would have to go back and forth from the lodge to try the dish. I continued trying each combination and eventually found the one that worked. There are four wires which makes a lot of different combinations. It was interesting working outside with a chill factor of minus thirty.

2/8

Sometime through the night the pipes in the bathroom froze and broke so during the day the broken pipes thawed out flooding the bathroom and out into the hall. It seems like there is constantly something new to deal with.

2/9

It is still snowing and blowing and I finally was sleeping sound when the dogs suddenly went into an explosion of barking sending my stomach into my throat. After that I was not able to go back to sleep and getting tired of tossing and turning decided not to fight it and got up to watch the storm. I could not see very much as the snow was falling so hard that it was causing white out conditions. It was pretty cool though and I enjoyed it. This morning the water coming into the lodge was frozen as the heat tape had come unplugged. Plugging it back in was all it took to correct its self which was a relief.

2/10

Today is my dad, Ray's birthday and I am missing him and my family.

The storm has finally passed leaving us with a calm clear day. The heater ran out of fuel and while Rick was using the Kubota to fill the diesel barrels the tractor quit running. This is almost getting comical. The fuel filter was clogged so he brought it in and cleaned it in the kitchen sink and now the sink is plugged.

Cowboy rolled in stinky fish again so he needed a bath. I was surprised that he found something fresh to roll in, as it has been so cold that everything lying around should be frozen. I should know by now that if it is out there, he will find it.

Pat radioed us several times but could not hear our response so assumed that the radio was acting up again but Sharon radioed from Nelson Lagoon stating that they were picking us up just fine so she then called Pat on the phone and he made the discovery that he had accidentally pushed the button on his radio for receiving. So all was back to normal, whatever that is.

2/11-12

I had trouble getting to sleep and as I lay tossing and turning shrews kept running back and forth in the room stealing dog food. That had the dogs very concerned and active so I finally gave up and got out of bed and the three of us went on a massive shrew hunt. I must admit, it was fun working with the dogs. I moved the furniture, the dogs would run the shrews down and pin them, and then I would attempt to make a slap kill with Rick's slipper. Usually unsuccessfully. If nothing else, it entertained us until five in the morning which was when I gave up on that game and tried to go back to sleep. The shrews did not quit and the dogs wanted to continue the game so I got back up, started the portable generator, turned on the TV, hoping the noise would drown out the sound of the critters. It worked and the dogs and I did not wake back up again until 9 am.

It was sunny and bright out when I awoke. That was nice after such a long night. Through the windows the sun gave the appearance of summer so I went out for a morning walk and the 1-degree temperature set me straight right quick. At one point Cowboy walked across the recently partially frozen lake while I held my breath. The thought of him breaking through the ice horrified me.

Cowboy on the Lake Ice

He crossed safely so I headed down to the Fish and Game cabin then followed along the backwaters and up Dump Hill. The ground is frozen which makes it much easier to go where I want. It was beautiful out as the sun glittered on the snow while the ice formations were spectacular. I could hear the water flowing under the ice and the sound is very loud at times as it rushes and gurgles. The ice in some spots is crystal clear and in others milky white. This evening the wind kicked up and the temperature went from 15 degrees up to 29 degrees within minutes. I went to bed being glad that I had gotten out and seen the sights before they changed. I expect by tomorrow, much of the frozen places will be melted and gone.

2/14

The wind continued to blow and I enjoy looking at the crushing ice as it breaks and flows into the river. I went out on the deck and the sound of the ice hitting the shores and rubbing against each other tinkled like a glass chandelier. It was quite soothing. I have not done much lately; except for study flying lessons. I have been spending six to eight hours a day at it, I am hooked. It is great to have enough time that I can spend doing something that I enjoy so much.

28

Horror Strikes

2/15/96

Rick has been staying up in the lounge most of the time only coming down to fix himself something to eat. He noticed several otters that came up river, into the lake to feed and brought it to my attention so that I could also watch them frolic and feed. There were six of them and they entertained us for hours with their playful nature and actions. The lake is partially frozen but has many holes broken in the ice, so the otters swim under the ice from hole to hole, and we never know where they will come back up. It is fun to watch them move. They run, run, run, and slide. It looks like fun.

Otter Tracks on the Lake Ice

The otters appear to playing a game of hide and seek, or tag. They also show off their fishing skills bringing fresh fish up on the ice to eat, which also brought in birds. Eagles, magpies, and ravens followed behind the otters fighting over the scraps and several times the eagles would fight with the otters attempting to take the catch from them. When the otters had their fill, they swam back down the river and were gone.

We decided to go for a walk so we crossed the river going over to take a closer look at the otter tracks on the ice. The dogs stirred up two fox and it was always exciting to watch them attempt to catch them. It would not be a good thing if they did. Even though the dogs double-teamed, the fox, as usual, they really did not had a chance. There are too many fox dens for the fox to dive into as well as they are much faster than the dogs and have mastered the art of darting

The ice at the end of the lake has been pushed by the wind into some fabulous formations and natural benches. I found one spot that fit me perfectly as a lounge chair, and I was resting there when I heard the dreaded barking of the dogs.

We suspected their quilled enemy had been found so we headed back to the lodge calling and whistling for the dogs to follow. When they did catch up to us Cowboy was full of quills. I was sick to my stomach. The quills were not only on the outside of his face but also on the inside of his mouth and inside his nose. He was a mess.

We returned to the lodge and began pulling. We pulled over a dozen quills out and it hurt him bad enough that he drew a line not allowing us to restrain him any longer. I radioed Arlene to see if she had any suggestions and she said that the way she sees it we have two choices. One was to take him across the runway (which meant, shoot him at the dump site) or the other was to hang him long enough for him to pass out then quickly pull the quills. I was horrified at both suggestions and would not consider either one. She explained that several people in the village had hung their dogs for the same reason and that it is certainly dangerous, but it could also save his life. I told her I could not do that.

She called a medic in Cold Bay and they suggested giving him Phenobarbital but no more than two tablespoons, one dose at a time. I tried that but even after the second dose; Cowboy was as alert as normal. The next thing that I decided to try was to get him drunk so I mixed vodka in canned tuna and he loved it. Four shots later he was drunker than a skunk and we were able to get a few more outer quills pulled but that sobered him up rapidly and he was fighting hard again. It was awful to see the intoxicated state that he was in and to watch him sway and stumble tore at my heart. He bumped into things and fell down, which became more than I could stand. Normally Cowboy is so precise and graceful and I felt responsible for getting him in this state where he was obviously humiliated and unhappy. I felt like crying, Rick started drinking the vodka and I was growing very impatient and sickened. I helped Cowboy up on the bed and stayed with him there through the night while he slept it off, hoping for a better day tomorrow.

2/16

It was a terrible day today as we attempted to restrain Cowboy. He will not allow it and is fighting us with everything he has, which is more than the two of us can match. I radioed Arlene again and asked her to call a vet for us hoping that they might have some suggestions. With the vet on the phone and me on the radio, Arlene relayed the questions and answers as the doctor had me list the medications that we had available. His suggestion was to use the morphine that was in the first aid kit and gave instructions on how to administer it. No more than four injections of 1/2 cc each. I gave him the first shot and as I stuck the needle into his thigh he freaked. A yelp came out of him that curdled my blood and as he jerked away it pulled the needle out before I was able to get the medicine dispensed. It turned into a horrible ordeal and took me four attempts to give him the first shot. I was now in tears. I had given my horses shots in the past and it is something I absolutely hate doing. I was a wreck. It took everything that I had in me to do this to my buddy while I tried to convince myself that I was helping him. The morphine was not reacting like we had hoped it would and I wound up giving him all four doses. The more I gave him the less he reacted to the shot itself appearing that he was not feeling the pain of the needle, but it never did get him to the relaxed state of mind, or asleep, so that we could work on him. I would lay with him, as he stayed motionless. The poor guy even drooled, but as soon as I moved or tried to get near his mouth he would sit up and act alert. I do not know how he was able to do that and for all the good it did, I wished that I had given the morphine to myself instead.

I radioed Arlene again and asked her to check on airfare for him and me so that I could take him to Anchorage to a vet. After some time, she radioed back informing me that it would cost five hundred dollars one way. That did not include the vet bill. I was devastated. This evening Theo and Little Allen radioed and talked to us for quite awhile. They were trying to comfort and convince us to try hanging Cowboy giving us instructions on exactly how to do it. I tried to consider it but just could not bring myself to it. They told us that at this point it was really our only choice. Cowboy was not eating or drinking and he just lies there crying. They were honest and told us that it is not a pretty sight, it is scary but felt that it would work.

I know that they sensed my feelings so Theo eventually stated that if the weather permitted, he and Little Allen would fly up the next day to help Rick do the deed, providing a way for me to remove myself from the ordeal. I was petrified to say the least.

2/17

Today was the most bizarre day of my life and I will never forget the horror. Arlene radioed around noon saying that Theo was going to fly in and she wanted me to fly back to the lagoon with him for a few days. I appreciated her concerns but could not leave Cowboy after all of this. I cannot express the feeling of relief when I heard the buzz of the plane, only to have it end abruptly in total disappointment. The airstrip was so slushy and soggy that after circling several times, Theo made the wise decision not to land. I understood but was crushed as I watched them fly away without landing. We are on our own. Cowboy had cried most of the night and I could not stand it any longer. I knew that something had to be done.

We attempted to make a harness and lift Cowboy off the ground hoping that without his footing he might not be able to fight us so hard but even with that we could not hold him still and the effort was useless. We had done everything we could think of and it failed. I knew what we had to do and said to Rick, "We have to hang him." He looked at me and knew that I meant it. I held my buddy and talked softly to him as I shuttered inside knowing that the action that we were about to take could kill him and that this could be my last moments with my faithful companion. Rick tied a strap to the rafter and put a sling around Cowboys neck as I turned my back not being able to watch. I timed Cowboy as he struggled and fought and was horrified at the sounds that were coming from him. He kept fighting for over a minute and at that point, something in me forced me to turn around, and I began talking and attempting to somehow comfort him. Shortly thereafter he passed out. He appeared dead and his tongue was blue. Trying to ignore the way he looked we rushed to get him down and pull the remaining quills that were in the roof of his mouth and his gums. I was surprised how soft the quills were and that they came out pretty easy. We worked while the shock of what we had just done was pulsing through my thoughts. Within seconds of finishing my buddy started to regain consciousness and I began to sob! I held him while he started waking up and looked at me. I have never been so thankful and relieved in all my life. In no time at all he seemed to be in pretty good shape and the job was done. I will never forget the horror and the memories that scare me. I took Cowboy out for a short walk and he stayed right by my side, which is unusual as he normally runs everywhere, checking things out. We came back inside and he drank a lot of water and other than tired, appears to be doing well. I radioed over to the Lagoon and told them the good news as they all cheered.

29

Better Days

2/18/96

Things are much better today even though I am still in a bit of shock or horror over what took place yesterday. I am however, very relieved and thankful that it turned out good. Cowboy is feeling much better today, his appetite is improving and he even felt like playing a little. I will give him a few days then check in his mouth to insure all is well.

2/19

A big storm blew in through the night bringing more snow and the chill factor went down to minus twenty with the 72-mph winds. Things banged and shook all night making it difficult to sleep. Cowboy and I listened as a four-legged animal ran past the lodge. It was probably a fox but I was surprised at how heavy footed it sounded as each step crunched on the ground. I suppose it could have been a wolf, which would make more sense, but we did not get the chance to see. By the time it was light out, the wind and snow had covered all tracks. Cowboy is doing well and seems to feel better each day. Time will heal us both.

2/20

The weather was very odd today. It seemed to change by the hour. The wind continued to blow, but one minute it would be sunny then the next minute the skies would darken and it would snow, at times, pretty heavy. Then the sun would come out again only to repeat the pattern. I guess it must be Alaskan spring showers. We have not had a mail or supply delivery for several weeks and have been out of eggs and butter for about that long as well. I am surprised at how little can be cooked without eggs. Theo radioed as it was finally a nice day in Nelson Lagoon and he was hoping to fly in but we had heavy winds and the airstrip is still in bad condition so I told him that I felt he should wait until the conditions improve. Amazing how different the worlds are around each bend.

I watched an ermine run around the yard today laughing at him while all of his movements are a hundred miles an hour, well so it looked. He runs back and forth between the lodge and the bunkhouse then I watched him catch a shrew and is now carrying it around as though he is not sure just what he wants to do with it. Funny fellow.

Late this afternoon I bundled up and went out to see if I could help break up the ice strip that runs the entire length of the airstrip. What a job.

2/21

Break up is continuing and as I took a walk along the backwaters and up over Dump Hill and I could not believe how full the waterways are. The water is raging and the dump is completely flooded. The lake has a strange effect to it today being turquoise in color from the reflection of the sky, yet has brown strips running through it. The brown is the sand stirring up from the bottom revealing how much the water is churning

2/25

The last few days have gone by fast. It has been quite awhile since we had a sunny day without wind. The sun came up at 9:15 and set at 6:30. We are gaining daylight rapidly. Rick took the Kubota out to the airstrip and spent several hours working in an attempt to divert the water off of the strip so it can dry out. A pool of water still runs the entire length of the strip and it freezes every night only to thaw and stand there every day. Landing a plane in this condition is out of the question. His efforts worked as the strip finally drained only to have the water flow to the lodge which is now flooded.

I spent the day with a shovel in hand digging and diverting the pool around the lodge to the culvert where it could flow into the lake. It felt good to be outside and working hard. It was so warm out that I did not need to wear a coat. What a change from the usual attire of bunny boots and a parka. The airstrip is clear of water but very soft so we are hoping for a couple of more nice days.

The ermine was out all day and the falcon was spotted as he harassed an eagle. Other than that, it is pretty quiet.

2/26

Theo radioed that he was on his way in. By now were we are also out of milk so the delivery was very welcomed. Our eggs did not come in so Pat sent over some commercial bags of liquid eggs. I was glad to get the staples. The wind came up this afternoon and got quite stormy. Winds blew from the south with gusts up to 60 mph. I was glad that the plane had made it in and got out in time. The rest of the day was spent going through the ever so welcomed mail.

2/27

The spring storm has continued and everything is flooding. The lake has risen over the banks and is up to the stairs, which lead up to the deck. Two days ago you could walk around the front of the dock the water level was so low and today the water is up over the top of the dock. I wanted to walk down to the Fish and Game cabin to take a look at things from the tower but could not cross the footbridge as the water is rushing over the top of it. I went back to the lodge and put chest waders then made my way down to the cabin, which was surrounded by raging water and was deep enough that I feared water was in the cabin as well. I did not attempt to open the door, as it would have flowed inside for sure. I climbed the tower and was amazed at the amount of debris and broken wood that are floating down stream and out to sea.

Flooded Fish & Game Tower

I watched the force of the water realizing that a person or animal would surely drown if they were unfortunate enough to get into it. Rick was cranky today and unintentionally I added fuel to the fire when I brought up the skiff that he left down at the spike camp.

2/29

The storm and breakup continued in full force and today and I noticed that the footbridge has now sustained damage from the rushing water. The water levels have gone down some but the bridge is not safe to use without making repairs on it. There are huge ice chunks left lying all across the tundra, which look rather odd and out of place.

It is leap year. Happy Birthday to all those who have to wait for this day to arrive.

3/3

The winds continue and the waves are crashing up over the dock. The landscape is changing from the raging waters and once again Mother Nature shows her powerful self. It would be nice to find a way to harness this power. I enjoyed watching the start of the Iditarod race this morning and like last year; Cowboy also sits and stares at the TV while the dogs bark anxiously waiting for their turn to run.

30

Stranded

3/4/96

The last two days were calm and clear and I brought up the idea of going down to the spike camp several times in an attempt to retrieve the skiff, wondering if it is even still there. I have been really concerned about it with the high and rough waters and even though I had nothing to do with taking the skiff down and leaving it, I cannot help but feel responsible for it and will not feel right until I know the skiff is still there and undamaged. Rick eventually grew irritated at me for bringing it up and as though he intended to prove me wrong he announced that we were both going down to check on it.

I was glad, as I just cannot settle without knowing. We made preparations, which included gathering supplies to last for a few days and I was thrilled to be in the skiff and heading down stream. We spotted lots of ptarmigan as we worked our way downriver. Their feathers are still white and they are still dumb.

The river is deep and erosion has changed the channels. It took several hours to finally make it to the cabin and to our dismay the motor was completely submerged. In fact, it had to be dug out from the gravel and sand that covered most of it. We feared that it might be a total loss but gained some relief to see that the skiff was still there. The small boat had been moving around and it was dented and scratched from the ice chunks and debris that slammed against the sides and over the top of it, but it was here. We are both thankful that the anchor had held for the most part but the grass that was tangled and woven around the rope showed the force that the water applied as it raged past.

It took both of us to carry the motor up to dry land and began examining it for damage. The motor was a mess. The cover was smashed and even though Rick had tied a tarp around it the sand and gravel had worked its way into it. It took several hours of work to clean it up and when Rick tried to pull the starting rope it would not even budge. We continued to attempt to clear the system and finally things loosened up and the rope pulled free. Fuel began to get through and after many attempts there was spark to the plug. Even with all of the positive signs we could not get the motor started. Not knowing too much about boat motors we did not even know if it could start after sustaining such damage and treatment. We doubted it, as logically it did not seem like it should.

We had hoped to each take a skiff back up river but as the day went on we knew that it was time to head back to beat the darkness. Rick loaded the motor in the skiff, tied the second skiff to the one we had come down river in and started back up stream at a very slow pace. It was a lot of work to expect the skiff to pull that much weight against the current. We barely got any distance before we realized that this was not going to work, and decided to take the damaged skiff back to the camp and secure it once again. I felt much better about leaving it now that I knew that it was at least safe and did not think the water would be that high again this year. We could always come back down and bring another boat motor to retrieve the skiff, so after the skiff was secured, we headed back to the lodge. Traveling was still very difficult against the swift current and then the jet boat motor started spitting and sputtering.

At one point, the dogs and I got out of the skiff and walked to lighten the load while Rick attempted to forge the river. It was just not working. We struggled to gain about 1/2 mile and with around ten or twelve miles to go, the situation appeared bleak. By now it was getting dark so we pulled the skiff to shore to talk about the options at this point and decided to go back to the cabin and spend the night hoping that the weather would hold allowing us to make another attempt in the morning. We also realized that we might have to leave both skiffs at the cabin and walk back to the lodge, which would be an all day event. I was really dreading that as I do not have boots or chest waders that really fit me as they are all too big on my feet meaning the walk would be miserable for me. We made it back to the cabin just as darkness fell upon us. We are wet, tired, and a bit scared.

I did not realize how cold I was until we got inside the cabin. I was thankful for the Colman propane heater that was there. We stripped down to dry our clothing and warm our bodies. The dogs shivered as they dried and we all shared two cans of chili and crackers for dinner. As we lay in the bunks trying to sleep we were silent as the thoughts of what the next day might bring rolled through our minds.

3/5

This morning we were both, surprisingly in good spirits even under the circumstances. We talked it over and decided to spend no more than two hours attempting to get one of the motors running. If we were not successful in that amount of time we would begin our journey, on foot, across the tundra. As soon as it was light outside we were down on the beach working with the jet motor. The problem appeared to be in the fuel system and it would run fine until you tried moving the boat at which time it would cut out and not have enough power. We decided that it would be of no use. Clouds were low and we could see fog working its way in from the Bearing Sea.

Not really having too much faith in the motor that had been buried, we made a few more attempts to get it running. After several attempts and to our amazement, it started! We cheered with excitement even though this did not mean it would get us home. We secured the cabin, wrapped the jet motor in the tarp and then struggled with the heavy weight of the motor as we carried it to the cabin. After the second skiff was dragged up onto the beach and anchored, we loaded the dogs and ourselves in the skiff in hopes of making it up stream.

We both held our breath and rode in silence as we rounded each bend, bringing us one curve closer to the lodge. Every mile we went, meant it was one less that we would have to walk. There were times that the water was too shallow for the prop so I would jump out of the skiff as Rick lifted the motor not wanting to shut it off while I struggled to pull the boat and him back into deeper water. Then I would have to jump back in the skiff on the move not wanting to lose any ground.

I have no idea where the strength came from for me to be able to do that, it was actually very amazing. We finally came to a point that we could see Bear Hill, which is directly across from the lodge and it was a sight to behold!

As we rounded the bend that brought the lodge into view tears welled up in my eyes. One last shallow had to be navigated through and I guess knowing that the lodge was in sight brought such relief that my strength was zapped and I could barely get back into the boat.

My legs felt bruised and sore from my toes to my hips and I had no energy left. We have never been so glad to beach the skiff and unload.

After a hot lunch and soak in the tub, I felt a great appreciation for the conveniences of the lodge, and again. There is no place like home.

31

Spring

3/6/96

Today we awoke to frozen fog, which made thankful that the storm held off until we returned to the lodge. This evening, the fog burned off so I walked down to the Fish and Game tower to assess the area after being gone over night. I am amazed how the water has changed the channels of the river. Places that were very deep are now shallow enough to walk across. The flooding is subsiding and the cabin withstood the challenge.

I could not stand Parti-girls dreadlocks any longer, she smells sour so we got the clippers and after two hours she looks a bit funny but smells much better. Parti-girl seems to be proud about her new look as she bounced around with delight. Maybe she can run faster.

Watching TV tonight we saw that Rick Swenson a twenty-year veteran to the Iditarod race had been ejected from the race as one of his dogs died on the trial. It is a new rule and Swenson is reacting to the decision badly. The thought of a dog dying just to win a race does disturb me even though I have seen how the dogs love to run. Athletes die while competing, but they love what they do.

The leading teams are making good time and are due into McGrath by tonight.

3/7

The weather continues to stay nice and even though the nights are cool the days are warm. While we were sitting out on the deck we came up with the idea to target practice using the .22 rifles so we tossed the decaying potatoes and onions into the water then shot and destroyed. It was fun but I noticed that his shooting has improved and I am not too sure if I like the fact.

3/8-9

The wind came up violently today and swamped the beached skiff. Rick got the tractor out and was able to drag it up the bank and even after another attack the skiff appears to be fine.

Snow flurries fell throughout the day reminding us that the harsh conditions that Alaska supports are always lurking.

The mildness allowed me to go out for a walk and I noticed the cross fox walking the shore across the river. It did not take the dogs long to spot it either. I have been avoiding going anywhere close to where the dreaded porcupine lives and that was the direction that the fox was heading. Both dogs crossed the river and now the fox was on the run with the dogs on its tail. Cowboy called off and I was relieved for that but Parti-girl did not, and continued with her chase. In time the fox had enough of being chased and stopped running only to turn on Parti-girl and have a skirmish with her. After several screams and yelps from them both she turned away defeated, and came back home. Her ear was bloody from a bite by the fox and I I am concerned about that.

3/12-13

Jeff King won the Iditarod race today and the celebration begins in Nome. Record times are being set this year.

I baked cookies all morning and even though the wind is still blowing and slushy snow is falling I went for a walk up the shores of the lake. I was thrilled to find six eagle feathers and I also gathered several beautiful duck feathers.

I walked along the lakeshore and came to an alder patch on the shore where several items are tied on the branches. The items included a beaded eagle feather, piece of glass, a bear tooth, and bird bones. As I stood there looking at the items it came to mind that this was in honor of Allen. I am astonished that I have not noticed it before now as I have walked past this spot many times.

3/14

This evening Theo radioed that he was going to fly in tomorrow, weather permitting, naturally.

3/15

I awoke with excitement; the day is calm and clear. The usual preparations were made for company and around 11:30 am I heard the buzz of the plane. This time Bill Johnson flew in with Theo. It was very enjoyable visiting with them. Bill is Prebin's father and has spent a great amount of time here at the lodge as well as in the area before the lodge was built. It was fascinating to listen to him talk about the history of the area. He stated the area was hunting grounds for the natives. Several people had been killed by bears right here in the location that the lodge now sits. Bill stated that Don had to get written permission from the natives of the village to build the lodge. Don kind of bribed them by flying in supplies, cigarettes, and liquor.

Bill told many ghost stories and shared experiences that he had himself here at the lodge. The people of the village are strong with their beliefs and superstitions and many of the people think that the lodge is haunted. Most of them will not stay here and many of them will not even come here.

Killing an animal is honored not something to be sold and used for trophy. I totally understand how they feel but I would not be staying here, having this awesome adventure, if it were not for Don and his family being able to support Bear Lake Lodge by charging people to come here.

The visit came to an end and when the plane was out of sight and could no longer be heard, the task of going through the mail and supplies was started. We received two dozen eggs, which was exciting as well as some fresh potatoes and oranges.

Later this afternoon we spotted a herd of caribou traveling our direction and Rick is keeping a close watch on them. I know what he is thinking but for me it was an awesome experience to see the herds coming through.

3/16

The day was spent watching the caribou herd as they wandered and feed on the tundra. We can spot them from a long distance away by their color standing out against the background.

The radio is giving us trouble again and I do not like losing communication. It is a strange emotion to know that no matter what might happen, there would be no way to contact anyone for assistance. The heater also went out but this time not from the cold but from the tank getting too low of fuel. Rick filled it and we are now down to our last 55-gallon drum of diesel.

3/17

A second larger group of caribou was spotted and our surroundings are coming to life. The calm day invited us to take a boat ride so we went to the head of the lake. The skiff was beached and we walked around noticing all of the new tracks in the sand. There are moose, wolf, and bear tracks. Knowing that the bear are up and moving is exciting for us to watch for. It would be fun to see some new born cubs before leaving this year. We worked our way along the shores of the lake and as we approached the yellow cabin we saw what the rushing waters had done to the supports. It will need to be repaired before it can be used. After our return to the lodge, I spent the rest of the evening watching herds of caribou until it was too dark to see.

3/18

Today started out very foggy but the fog burned off and became a beautiful day. The radio is still only working off and on and while I was talking with Arlene, we were cut off and could not reconnect.

The caribou are still in the area and I attribute that partly to Cowboy staying close to home and not discovering them yet. I spotted a young bull attempting to herd a cow as she tried to get back to the main herd. The young calves are cute as they run, jump, and frolic about. We also saw a moose across the lake. It is really fantastic to see all the animals and the area come to life after such a long quiet season.

3/21

A few more days have passed and I walked down to the Fish and Game tower to try and get a better look at the caribou herds. Cowboy headed out in the direction of the caribou and as I whistled to call him back the caribou also heard me and began running towards me, which was a big surprise. They stopped and looked before going back to eating.

I was also excited to see green grass growing in several patches. I walked the shores of the lake and was thrilled to find four eagle feathers. Three mature feathers and one immature. They are all very beautiful and so special to me.

3/24

The night was calm and clear and I spent much of the evening on the deck with the spotting scope looking at the stars, moon, and Hails Comet. Without lights from a city the night skies are fabulous here and the comet can be seen very well.

3/26

Recently I have been spending time each day in preparation for my departure. Either Warren or John will be here any day to bring in supplies and take me back to the peninsula. I will fly to Portland from there to see my family again while Rick spends the last couple of weeks here at the lodge by himself like we did last year.

As hard as it is to leave this place I am anxious to see my family and friends.

I watched an eagle catch a dolly varden and fly off with it. Two of the caribou herds have joined together and make an impressive sight. The herds continue to come closer to the lodge and Rick is going out and stalking them. He wants to see just how close that he can get to them.

Today we ran out of dog food so I made a concoction of hamburger, rice, and oatmeal. The dogs love it and of course are not complaining.

3/27

Another small herd of caribou showed up coming from the valley behind Dump Hill. Rick set out after them but they were on the move and he was several hours behind them. Even though I am not thrilled with his motives I am glad to see Rick get outside.

We have still been able to see the comet each night and are enjoying that.

3/28

I spent the day on the deck basking in the warmth of the sun. It is nice to have summer clothes on and no shoes. While scanning the mountains and hillsides with the scope I spotted an exposed den, which looked very large in size. Just thinking about looking into a bear cave fascinates and attracts me.

3/29

Today Rick went out again now obsessed with getting a caribou and after several hours radioed me with the hand held radio announcing that he wanted me to bring the ranger out. I knew that meant that he had successfully made a kill. I was not real happy while I prepared and headed out across the tundra to find him.

He was about two miles out so the fun of the day was the challenge of maneuvering through the water and swamps as I made my way across the tundra. I could see him from quite a distance away. I helped him load the meat and we headed back toward the lodge. After we crossed the backwaters the ranger broke a gear and came to an abrupt halt.

Rick walked to the lodge and retrieved the Kubota tractor and we pulled the wounded ranger back to the hanger. I helped him skin the caribou and hang the meat up in the meat cache. He cleaned the hide the best he could then tied it to the dock so it could float in the river to wash it before drying it.

It was nice that six moose were spotted this evening in different locations around the lodge. As always, it is a thrill to watch the wildlife.

3/31

We spent the day in the skiff patrolling the shores of the lake and a very large set of bear tracks were discovered at the head of the lake. It could be the same bear that we tracked last fall. His paw print is much larger than my boot print, which is not small. I would sure like to see that bear.

We were almost back at the lodge when we saw a plane in the air. Our first thought was it was my ride out but the closer we got to each other we realized that it is a plane that we are not familiar with. It landed on the strip and a man named Bill and his friend Frank waited for us to dock. They are from King Cove and were out enjoying the nice weather deciding to stop by Bear Lake Lodge and see how the winter has treated us. They had fresh butter clams with them and gave us more than enough to enjoy a good meal.

The strange thing about the visit is I felt an uneasy about them for some reason. I am glad we were close to the lodge when they landed.

4/2

I spent six hours cutting and wrapping caribou meat. Rick does not know how to cut and I suggested he allow me to deal with it as he was making a mess of things. I do not mind this part of hunting; in fact, I would prefer to handle my own meat as I am picky about cutting off all fat, tendons and membranes. The meat taste better to me prepared that way.

Tonight we received word that John would be out the next day to get me. A lump rose in my throat as the words came over the radio.

32

Final Departure

4/3/96

The big day arrived and the weather looked good only to get worse as the day went on. Several times someone attempted to radio us but we could not hear much except for static. During one attempt we plainly heard the sound of an airplane engine. We assumed it was John and I prepared to leave the lodge. The snowstorm continued and we were surprised when the plane broke through the clouds and landed on the airstrip.

Because of the storm we rushed to unload the plane then load my things into it. There was no time to get all mushy about leaving. I strapped myself in and quietly cried as we taxied and lifted up into the air. I was unhappy and scared about leaving the life that I genuinely loved. I believed that this would be my last time here at Bear Lake Lodge and saying good-bye to the wonderful lodge, the land, and the people, was very difficult for me.

We headed toward the Bearing Sea; I did the best I could to keep a grip on my emotions. It helped that the storm cleared and I was able to enjoy the sights as we flew across the tundra towards the ocean. We spotted a bear not too far out from the lodge and from there lots of caribou and birds were seen. It was beautiful to see the tree line at King Salmon and as we entered into Lake Clark Pass the sky grew dark and gray. The wind also picked up so John went up to a higher elevation searching for some smoother air. I asked him if he would like me to take it from here; he laughed at my joke. By the time we left Lake Clark Pass and crossed the Cook Inlet we were getting tossed around pretty good and the visibility was also bad. Snow was falling hard and it was getting dark. The G.P.S. unit in the plane was critical today and did the job of bringing us in safe. All was endured and we made a perfect landing at the Kenai Airport.

Warren was waiting for us and helped transfer my things to his truck then took me out to a nice prime rib dinner.

Now the task of getting re-adjusted to life, in so-called civilization begins. I will be flying to Oregon tomorrow and when my visit there is completed I will be returning to Alaska and at this point, I have no idea what my next adventure will be.

ABOUT THE AUTHOR

I was born in California and have lived in Oregon, Idaho, Montana and Alaska. Always having a sincere affection and attraction for the outdoors and wildlife I have enjoyed many "once in a life time" type adventures involving these topics.

I would say that I have a good since of humor and have never been afraid to try something new. This story is based on my daily journal while care taking at a remote hunting lodge in solitude, on the Alaskan Peninsula. My husband, dog and I were there for a total of 14 months. It was an amazing experience even though at times it was scary, sad and complicated. I feel my story openly reflects the joy and the hardships that one is challenged with in this type of life. I hope that you enjoy reading about this adventure, I am grateful to have had the chance to live it. The experience has changed my life forever.

-penny nickle